EARTH
PRESENTS

EARTH PRESENTS

HOW TO MAKE BEAUTIFUL GIFTS FROM NATURE'S BOUNTY

BY BEVERLY PLUMMER

A & W Visual Library

*The author wishes to express appreciation for permission to quote
in these pages from the following books:*

New Mexico Village Arts *by Roland F. Dickey*
The University of New Mexico Press, Albuquerque, New Mexico
Copyright 1949, © *1970 by Roland F. Dickey*

The Book of Country Crafts *by Randolph Wardell Johnston*
A. S. Barnes & Company, Inc., Cranbury, New Jersey
Copyright © *1964, 1966, 1970*

Survival Arts of the Primitive Paiutes *by Margaret M. Wheat*
The University of Nevada Press, Reno, Nevada
Copyright © *1967 by University of Nevada Press*

Natural Dyes in the United States *by Rita J. Adrosko*
Smithsonian Institution Press, Washington, D. C.
Copyright © *1968*

*And to the Hudson's Bay Company for permission to reproduce a photograph
of an Eskimo carving.*

Designed by Kathleen Carey

Printed in the United States of America
Published by arrangement with Atheneum

John Plummer created the drawings of the earth presents, and John and Beverly worked together on the photographs of them.

Unless noted otherwise, all the objects in this book were made by the author.

CONTENTS

The Earth Itself

Earth-Born Things

Earth Walkers

Flyers, Swimmers, Fallers & Other Small Performing Artists

EARTH
PRESENTS

THE EARTH ITSELF

Fieldstones, Skipping Stones, Pebbles and an Occasional Boulder

OF ALL the good things lying around on the earth waiting to be put to use, stones are more plentiful than any other material except dirt. In the contemporary world, they are largely ignored, but there were times in history when stones were a part of almost every human activity. Mexicans used them for grinding fruits and seeds, for scrapers, mortars, and jugs. On the island of Yap, huge white stones resembling wheels were legal tender. Eskimo craftsmen made lamps, weapons and cooking pots from them. Early settlers in New England built unmortared fences that still do their job today. And all good wilderness hikers know that if

they hold a stone in their mouth when they're
thirsty, they'll feel like they've had a cool drink of
water.

Fieldstones, skipping stones, pebbles and plain
old boulders are the proletariat of the rock world.
They're uninhibited, uneducated, rough, tweedy
and scarred with a terrible kind of beauty. Color
isn't normally associated with them, yet it could
be, for they are as variously hued as wildflowers.
A handful of small stones casually picked from a
driveway in upper Wisconsin will reveal slivers
of glossy black, dull red and sharp flashes of green
and blue. Every part of the country has its own
unique rock formation due to the fact that the
earth is constantly moving and reshaping itself. It
doesn't move as fast as an interstate bus or a maple
leaf, but it moves just the same. Rivers cut. Fault
lines shift. And trees fall just as they've done for
centuries. This means that when you decide to
give a rock for a gift, you're giving something that
took millions of years to form. If you want to
think about this in awe-inspiring terms, consider
the fact that granite, one of the hardest of all stones,
once churned and bubbled like soup.

One of the best features of a stone's character
is the fact that it has no "good" or "bad" side for
viewing. The ones with the dimension of a small
melon look very much at home scattered about in
a living room. I call them floor sculptures. You
can give them in a parcel of one to three (though

it's not good to be this arbitrary). So much depends upon your mood at the time and the kind of person you want to present with such a gift. I have a dozen or so that I change about periodically. Sometimes they're heaped together in a clump. At other times they get separated when guests pick them up to hold. It's good to see this interaction between the stones and the guests. Traditional pieces of sculpture don't ask to be picked up and stroked. The stones do. In fact, some of them almost *demand* it. There's one pink one that's grown quite pushy—in a tranquil kind of way.

Last summer I found a green wedge-shaped rock reaching out of the bank of a country road. The section exposed to the air had grown a patch of deep green moss. Under the dirt, when I brushed it away, I found a strip of white quartzy material running across the tip end and down one side. It didn't look like a rock that would care to live inside, so I gave it to a friend for her garden.

On the southern shore of Lake Superior, where people normally hunt for agates and other semiprecious stones, there's a spot called Little Girl's Point. The beach there is made up of infinite layers of flat, palm-sized stones. They range in color from the far side of white to the other side of blue. Some come with one pale line slightly raised or incised into the deep color of the stone. Nothing needs to be done to them that the lake hasn't already done. They can lie along a kitchen window sill to keep company while carrots are being scraped. A group can be arranged in a wooden bowl or around the base of a large potted plant. They look fine on a coffee table too, where they will sit on letters until the mailman comes. Small ones can be given away in a bowl of sand, to be displayed like flowers.

The Japanese know about the wisdom in stones. They have been using them in their gardens for centuries. The most famous example is the garden of Ryoan-ji in Kyoto. There is no vegetation—just a huge area of raked sand with groupings of stones, fifteen in all, that appear to be islands in a sea. The Japanese actually shop for stones, as we do for plants. There are stores that sell stones ranging in size from pebbles to two-ton boulders. I don't know how you could give someone a gift of a two-ton boulder, but it's nice to think about. Especially if it had cracks or fissures in it that would support the growth of small plants. It's much easier, though not half so challenging, to envisage gifts of pebbles. Several handfuls will fill a glass container, and they look handsome in a spot where the sun can shift around them (Figure 1). They spread colors like a stained-glass window. Intermediate-sized pebbles can be used to simulate a stream bed in a garden. It takes a sizable number to do this, but it would be exciting to consider it as an ongoing gift, as you would a magazine subscription. Think of it—giving someone a stream,

FIGURE 1 *Displaying pebbles in water releases their inherent warmth of color.*

a section at a time!

Some people I know carry lemon drops or jelly-beans in their pockets. And I've read about a lady who always carries wildflower seeds when she goes out driving. When she comes upon a desolate-looking roadside she tosses the earth the makings of a stand of daisies or red poppies. One good person I know carries pebbles in his pocket. He keeps them warm and comfortable until he encounters someone who would appreciate a smooth pebble—if it's a stranger, so much the better. Of course, they're not gift wrapped; they're presented just as is.

If you would like to give pebbles as gifts but are too shy to do it his way, you might want to make a drawstring bag from some honest fabric like canvas or Indian Head. Fill it with an assortment of seven or twelve skipping stones. The givee would wear it tied to his belt until he reached a small pond or lake, at which time he could do the skipping. A present that can be used is a fine thing.

Everyday Stones, Slightly Altered

Everyday stones will respond to imagination and ingenuity by turning into unusual gifts. Think about the stones you normally see around you, or those you've observed on vacations. Go on a rock hunt. Bring some home. Live with them a little while until they tell you what it is they'd like to be. Trust them. It may take a little time for the message to come through, but it will happen. If you don't hurry them, you'll find that your desires and those of the rocks will turn out to be harmonious.

The Eskimos had a good way with fieldstones. They used them for tools, amulets to ward off evil, mortars, bowls and lamps. In fact, one of the most bewitching marriage customs I know is the one in which an Eskimo bride brought a lamp to her husband. The lamp symbolized everything she hoped to bring to the marriage—strength, warmth and light. The bowl-shaped lamp was hollowed at the center and filled with fat pounded from animal tissue. A moss wick extended from the center to a flat rim along the edge.

It would be a simple matter to make a contemporary modification of this lamp for a bride's gift. Start with a stone that already suggests the shape of a bowl and is the color and texture you prefer. Hollow out the center with a mallet and chisel. It doesn't have to be deep. A saucerlike indentation is enough. Try to find a stone that is very close to the shape you want, because fieldstones can be stubborn and unpredictable. Test the rock for cracks by pouring water over it. Water will darken the stone at the crack lines. Test it for soundness by tapping with a hammer. You should hear a ringing sound, not a thud.

Rough out a hollow with a chisel and mallet and then refine the shape with files. The gift of a lamp can be accompanied by a bottle of the oil sold

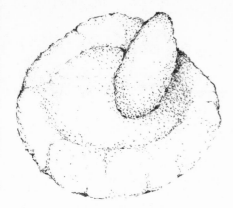

FIGURE 2 *A rough fieldstone about 6 inches across makes a handsome mortar when a bowl-shaped indentation is carved in its surface.*

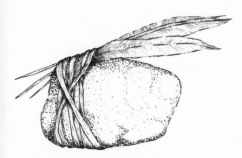

FIGURE 3 *A frog emerges from a rock of the same basic form and dimensions. This little Zuni fetish is a part of the collection of the Anthropology Department, Northern Illinois University, DeKalb, Illinois.*

today for use in old-fashioned lamps. It is scented, but you can add your own scent too. A wick can be made from the heavier wicking sold for use in candlemaking. If you want to modify the lamp even more, fill the hollow with candle wax, give it a candle wick, and then explain that the wax can be replaced as it is burned.

To make a mortar such as the Eskimos used, a blocky, sturdy rock would be best. The hollow will need to be deep enough to accomodate the material to be ground, plus a pestle (Figure 2). It can be used for grinding fresh peppercorns, dried parsley, and the bark and stems of plants that yield teas and cooking herbs.

Some stones already carry a strong suggestion of an animal form. The Zuni Indians often carried small stone fetishes that resembled frogs (Figure 3). For them, the frog represented rain. "Fetish" sounds like a threatening word until you consider that technically it means "an inanimate object regarded with awe as being the embodiment or habitation of a potent spirit." You may know someone to whom you'd like to give the potent spirit of a lion, the quickness of a fox, or the grace of a gull. You can try to do this by creating an amulet or a charm that would be worn as a necklace. Or make a fetish to sit wherever its good vibrations can best be felt.

Think carefully about these magic things before you begin to make them. If you make a lion, think about what a lion is like. Then think what *this* lion is like. Is he a grouch? Do his feet ever hurt? Is he kind to his family? What do you want the lion to say to your friend? When you have this all figured out, look over your stones and see which one looks like there might be a lion in it waiting to get out. Help it by carving away appropriate spots or by adding string, beads, feathers or even another stone.

Here is a brief list of other ways stones have been used (Figure 4): (*a*) A nest of baby owls is made from walnut-sized rounded stones. Eyes, and the suggestion of feathers and beak, are painted on the stone with enamel and then thinly sprayed with lacquer. (*b*) Unusually shaped or colored stones are bound with leather and worn as a pendant. (*c*) Flat stones with rounded edges (found along shorelines of large lakes or where rivers have been) are piled one on top of the other in a tower sculpture. A reliable flat stone makes the sturdy support at the base. Each new stone is glued on top of the previous one with white glue and allowed to dry before the next one is added. (*d*) Beautiful small pebbles and shards are laced with thin strips of leather and then hung from branches as a mobile.

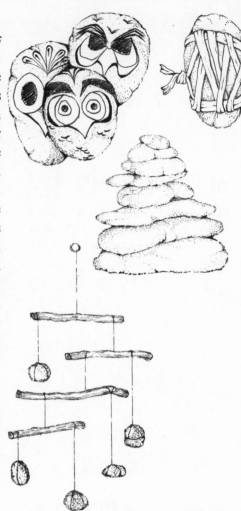

FIGURE 4 *Ordinary stones become special when they're painted, bound with strips of leather, or combined with other rocks.*

Soapstone and Alabaster

SOAPSTONE

Soapstone is so soft that you can shape it with a pocket knife or a file. And it's not hard to find when you know what to look for. Oftentimes it lies loose and neglected in an open field—easy to overlook because it appears to be so ordinary. And that's probably one of the most insulting statements you can make about anything. Ask a dozen people which they'd rather be—ordinary or ugly —and I'd guess that at least ten of them would choose to be ugly. I don't like to believe that soapstone in its natural state is ordinary, but I'm afraid it is. It looks gray and shabby and just a little tired. But in its heart it knows better. It must grin to itself, like one of those celebrities who hide their identity with everyday clothes and hair curlers. For when you take a piece of soapstone home and rub away its dusty surface, it explodes into life. Flakes of color appear that run from misty green to a deep mysterious black. They pour over each other like scales on a mountain trout. And lines course between the flakes like an intricate capillary system designed to water the stone and keep it fresh. Let other people hunt for turquoise or opals. Soapstone has a sense of humor and I want it for my friend.

Soapstone is mined today as talc for all kinds of industrial purposes—rubber, insecticides, roofing materials and paper. It is not much prized as an art material. At one time in history, though, it was used for body ornaments, beautiful bowls and perfume jars. A group of agricultural people in Sierra Leone carved fat little figures from it which they charged with the task of bringing them a good harvest. And Indians in North America sculpted it into bowls and pipes.

But the Eskimo seems to have found a deeper, more spiritual relationship with this stone than any other group. The figures they carve, even today, pulse with energy. They're like pieces of fruit ready to burst (Figure 5). The Eskimo's religion told him that everything in nature—the trees, the sun, man, the wind—all had an inner spirit, an "innua." And stones, along with polar bears, had the most powerful innua of all. The artist not only respected the stone but took care to understand it thoroughly before attempting to carve anything from it. A man sometimes carried a stone for months before beginning to work with it. His tools were simple because soapstone is very malleable. He used carving tools of stone or bone and then polished the piece with another stone. To bring out the color he rubbed it with blubber.

Bobby Takrik, a contemporary artist, carves with only a file and a pocket knife—tools not too far removed technologically from the ones used by his ancestors. But he still follows the old custom of taking time to let the stone decide what it wants to be. He keeps it close until he's absolutely certain of the form that lies within. Then it just takes

FIGURE 5   *"Eskimos Washing" by Charlie Seeguapik, a contemporary piece of soapstone sculpture. (Photo courtesy of Hudson's Bay Co., Winnipeg, Manitoba.)*

one hour for him to carve a figure. It takes another hour to polish it.

Because soapstone is so soft, it imposes almost no restrictions on the craftsman. It is, in fact, the softest of all stone and can be scratched with the fingernail. Only the simplest tools are needed. Children enjoy it because the figures in their mind can be translated almost immediately into a work of art. It's an excellent way for them to discover they can combine their imagination with a fragment of the earth.

Gifts from Soapstone. Tranquilizer, or worry stone (Figure 6, right), is silky and warm. To carry one is to feel the order of the universe, for a stone doesn't represent order, it is order. No one knows for certain how it works, whether the bad vibrations from your body flow into the stone and are eaten up, or whether the good vibrations from the stone rush out and overpower the bad. Whatever is involved, people who carry them say they're more effective than shouting and a lot healthier than pills. Any piece of soapstone would be happy to be put to such a use.

Scrap of soapstone about 2″ x 2″ x ½″, paste wax, No. 120 grit sandpaper, No. 200 wet and dry paper, file.

WORRY STONE (Figure 6)
MATERIALS AND TOOLS

1. Hold chunk of stone in hand, turning it as you work. Rub with a file until the shape you want begins to appear. Any comforting shape is fine—square, round or irregular.

2. When it is shaped as you wish it, smooth it with sandpaper. Final sanding should be done with wet and dry paper, dipped occasionally into water. When it glistens and feels silky smooth, it is ready for waxing.

PROCEDURE

FIGURE 6 *Necklace, left, and worry stone, right. Both were made from soapstone scraps. The author added melon seeds dyed various shades of green and gold. Feathers are gold also.*

3. Apply three coats of paste wax. Allow each coat to dry thoroughly and buff with a soft cloth before next coat is applied.

Chunk of soapstone roughly 4″ in length from which a slab of soapstone can be cut, four small scraps of soapstone for chunky beads, three bone beads, dyed fruit or vegetable seeds, six feathers (from a craft shop), two strips of leather lacing 12″ long (from a shoe repair or leathergoods shop), bead string, sandpaper, paste wax, glue, hacksaw, drill with assorted small bits.

1. Saw one piece for the pendant roughly measuring 2″ x ½″ x ½″ (Figure 7).

2. Select four small pieces roughly 1″ x ¼″ x ¼″, and drill a hole in each of them with small bit (for stringing). Drill hole in pendant for stringing.

3. Drill hole at bottom of pendant through which the leather lacing and feather decoration will pass.

4. Leaving some surfaces rough and unpolished for textural variety, sand and polish all the stones as in directions for worry stone, pages 14–16.

5. Draw the two strips of leather lacing through the hole in bottom of pendant, half the length hanging in front and the other half behind. You now have four ends. Cut off one of these lengths an inch below pendant and use the length to bind the other strips together, as in Figure 6. Wind it

NECKLACE *(Figure 6)*
MATERIALS AND TOOLS

PROCEDURE

FIGURE 7 *When sawing a soft stone, keep elbow, hand and saw in one straight line. This will keep the saw from twisting and breaking the piece. Use a gentle stroke rather than a muscular one.*

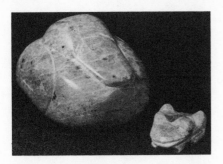

FIGURE 8 *Duck, left, is 3 inches high and smoothly polished. The shape of an existing stone suggested the tiny frog, right. He is only 1½ inches tall and is unpolished. (By John Plummer.)*

tightly around the strips, glue in place, and cut off length you don't need.

6. String a bone bead on each of the three strips. Stick the quill ends of two feathers up inside each bead and then wind a short length of lacing around the stem of the feathers. Glue in place.

7. String the seeds, four stone beads and pendant on bead thread, using the design shown or one of your own choosing. The seeds can be squash, pumpkin, melon, gourd, etc. They are soaked overnight in liquid dye and are strung while still soft and pliable.

OBSERVATIONS: Any beads you might have on hand can be used, or beads can be purchased. Any handsome cord can be substituted for the leather lacing. A hand drill can be substituted for an electric one.

FROG AND DUCK (Figure 8)
MATERIALS AND TOOLS

One piece of soapstone roughly 5″ x 3″ x 3″, and one piece 1″ x 1″ x 2″, sandpaper, wet and dry paper, paste wax, file, rasp.

PROCEDURE

The artist studied the rough stones for several days before deciding what form would be best for them. Since each rough chunk of stone is different, it wouldn't be fair to try to give explicit directions for a particular figure for you. In general terms, though, what you would do is this: Consider the stone. Also consider the fact that when you cut into a stone, *any* stone, you are looking at a part of the earth that no one has ever seen before. It will slow your hand and quicken your heart. When you and the stone have reached an understanding, you may want to make a pencil sketch to help firm the idea in your mind. Then take a rasp and begin to take away the stone's unwanted portions. As the shape gradually emerges and is refined, you can switch to a file, which doesn't go quite as quickly. It is better not to try to work too fast. Let the stone resist a little. Allow it to push back against your file. Use a file (or pocket knife) to further refine the shape or incise it with sharp lines. Polishing is up to you. The little frog was left very rough because the artist thought he looked happier that way. Use polishing directions as for the worry stone, page 14.

Sources for Soapstone. Soapstone lies free in many places in the country. Look for a chunky, dusty gray stone. In the country where I was able to find it, it lay in a farmer's field in free-standing chunks that weighed from two or three pounds to over twenty pounds. When you go "prospecting" for any stone, it will be good to remember that minerals are not a replaceable material like the grass or the trees. What we have is all we'll get. So we must all be kind. The Paiute Indians believed that when they took a gift from the earth they should return the favor. So they always left a little present behind when they harvested anything—whether they were picking grasses or gathering bark from the trees. You might feel foolish doing this, but it wouldn't hurt to hum the earth a little tune or give it a loving pat with your hiking boot. We must be kind too to the owner of the land where the rock is found. All land today is owned by someone and no matter how free the stone looks, it would only be fair to ask permission to carry it away.

Soapstone appears in noncommercial quantities in many states—among them, New York, Wisconsin, Oregon and Georgia. There are several ways to determine where to look. The Department of the Interior, Bureau of Mines, Washington, D.C. 20240, publishes a list of state geologists. A letter to the appropriate geologist explaining your wishes will bring information about deposits or mines in the area you wish to explore. Most states also have rock and mineral clubs whose members can be good sources of information. State tourist bureaus and local chambers of commerce will know what rocks and minerals are present in their area.

An excellent source of soapstone is the scrap heap of the large talc mines in California, Nevada, Arkansas, Virginia and Washington. There are smaller mines in other states too. At this time, many of the mining companies allow visitors to go in and choose pieces of stone in a quantity for carving. Information about the mines can be obtained from the same sources already mentioned. There is one thing to remember when accepting the kindness of the mine owners: be sure to follow their safety rules.

If it isn't possible to "prospect" for it personally, soapstone is quite inexpensive to buy. Fifty cents a pound is roughly what pieces cost. This means that a good-sized chunk can be bought for under five dollars. It should make one large gift or a half dozen small ones such as the duck and frog. Stores that sell artists supplies carry it, as do the rock and mineral shops listed in the yellow pages of your telephone directory. The Department of the Interior, Bureau of Mines, also publishes a list of rock and mineral dealers.

ALABASTER

Alabaster, a compact form of the mineral gypsum, gleams with shades of pink, yellow, brown or black, and sometimes a combination of all of these. When a piece is polished it becomes almost translucent—as though one could poke a finger through it. Every finished piece looks like it must have spent time in a treasure chest. Apart from its beauty, alabaster has several good things going for it. It's soft and extremely easy to carve. On a hardness scale of one to ten, it rates a two—just one step up from soapstone. And it's easy to find. Most times it's free.

The name itself has an elegant ring and history reveals that it once consorted with royalty. Roman, Greek and Egyptian artists carved perfume jars, jewel boxes and bottles from it. Reliefs in alabaster decorated palaces in such ancient places as Nimrud,

Khorsabad and Nineveh. It is a splendid stone when put to such uses and a practical one when it's not. In early New Mexico, Indian women baked gypsum rocks, pounded them into powder, and made a soupy paste to plaster their adobe walls. This "yeso" dried to a glistening, dazzling white. Religious artists of that time spread thin coats of yeso over slabs of seasoned pine or cottonwood to make smooth surfaces for their paintings. Artists today still use this material.

General Directions for Working with Alabaster. To shape alabaster, use the sawing directions in Figure 7. To smooth and polish it, use directions for the worry stone on page 14. Generally speaking, alabaster and soapstone can be handled the same except for the following instances: (1) Alabaster will sometimes crack or break along a seam. So before you work with it, drop it on the floor or table. It's better to have breaks occur at this point rather than after hours of work. Save the chips or nuggets that break off. They can be drilled and shaped into small, ancient-looking beads and then strung into a necklace. (2) The softer, less compact form of alabaster shouldn't be used for anything meant to hold water or other liquid. It will dull or possibly disintegrate if it is subjected to liquid over prolonged periods of time. (3) Polyurethane varnish can be substituted for paste wax to put the final touches on alabaster. It gives a much higher gloss and serves to protect the surface.

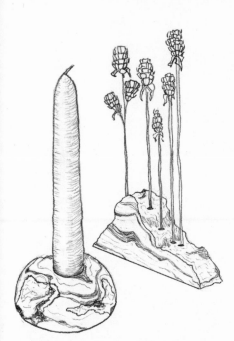

FIGURE 9 *The candleholder, left, and weed pot, right, were carved from one chunk of alabaster salvaged from a mine dump in California. The stone is almost pure white striped with puddles of pink and pale green.*

Rough chunk of stone about the size of your fist, No. 120 grit sandpaper, No. 200 wet and dry paper, polyurethane varnish, file, drill with ⅛″ bit.

1. Drop stone to check for cracks or breaks.
2. Using the file, flatten one area of the stone to act as bottom surface of container.
3. Drill set of random holes down through the body. You may drill clear through or stop before you reach the bottom.
4. Smooth body of pot with sandpapers. Finish with varnish, using directions given on the container.
5. Arrange dry weeds or flowers in the holes.

A stone roughly the size of a large apple, No. 120 grit sandpaper, No. 200 wet and dry paper, polyurethane varnish, drill with bits ranging from ⅛″ to 1¹¹⁄₁₆″, file.

1. Drop stone to check for cracks, etc.
2. Using a file, smooth one surface for the base.
3. Starting with the ⅛″ bit, drill one hole down through center of stone. Using a larger bit each time, gradually enlarge the hole until it will hold a normal-sized dinner candle. This is 1¹¹⁄₁₆″.
4. Smooth some areas; leave others rough.
5. Brush varnish over the smooth areas by following directions on can. Leave rough areas unpolished.

WEED POT (Figure 9)
MATERIALS AND TOOLS

PROCEDURE

CANDLEHOLDER (Figure 9)
MATERIALS AND TOOLS

PROCEDURE

FIGURE 10   *Alabaster and bead necklace. In the center is a piece of rough gypsum and a ring formed of the same material.*

A chunk of alabaster roughly the size of a large orange, twenty-two miscellaneous beads, handful of small glass beads, clasp from a discarded necklace, bead string, glue, No. 120 sandpaper, No. 200 wet and dry paper, paste wax, file, hacksaw, drill with ⅛″ bit.

NECKLACE (Figure 10)
MATERIALS AND TOOLS

1. Drop stone to check for breaks and then place solid piece in vise (see Figure 7). Saw two slices ¼″ thick. Turn these slices and saw them into two rectangular beads ¼″ wide by 2″ long, and two beads ¼″ wide by 1″ long. You now have four beads.

2. Drill hole in top of each bead for stringing.

3. Refine shape of beads with a file and then further refine them with sandpaper.

4. Polish and wax, as for the worry stone, page 16.

5. Thread all beads as shown in Figure 10, or create your own design. Secure the clasp to each end of string, knotting it carefully and placing a drop of glue on the knot.

Sources for Alabaster. Depending on the geographical area, alabaster (gypsum) either is found at the surface or is brought out of the earth by machinery. It is mined for a variety of industrial uses, and the mining areas are where you will be able to get stone for your use. Mines have dump heaps that visitors can sort through. Large mines

PROCEDURE

are located in Michigan, New York, Texas, Ohio, California and Iowa, but gypsum is found in other states too. Use the same methods for tracking it down as were described for soapstone (pages 18–19). When you locate a mine, be sure to write or call to ask permission to visit and to learn what their safety requirements are.

If you don't want to "prospect" for it yourself, alabaster can be purchased from art supply houses and from mineral shops listed in the yellow pages. Since it's plentiful, the cost is quite reasonable.

Finding and Harvesting Almost-Gems

The earth is covered with rocks and minerals. We kick them around all the time—or ignore them. I love some of their names: jasper, psilomelane, silkstone, rodochrosite. Many of them, because of their color and structure, are so beautiful that they can be appreciated as gems. Since there are so many, I'm going to choose just three to describe here. They will give you an idea of what's available—and free. Then if you get really turned on to "prospecting," there are books listed in the appendix to lead you further.

AGATES

Agates (Figure 11) are as various as wildflowers and just as difficult to describe in a few words. They come in every size from pebbles to oranges.

In a few rare instances they're monstrously large —the size of a bushel basket. The color most often found is a caramel brown with bands of red and cream. Sometimes agates have to be opened before their beauty is apparent. Sawing them in half reveals whorls and ripples of frozen energy, as though whole rivers had been compacted into this ingeniously small space. If you like, you can believe any of several folk tales about agates. Some people say they will heal the bite of a scorpion. Others say you can improve your vision by holding one each day and studying its contours. These curious stones are turned up by pounding waves along Lake Superior's shoreline in Michigan and Minnesota. They're also found in Oregon, Pennsylvania, Montana and other states as far apart as Texas and Connecticut.

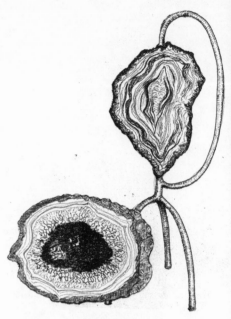

FIGURE 11 *Geode, foreground, is open to show a crystalline cavity lined with blue. The agate mounted on the stand has layers of pink, pale brown and dark brown.*

GEODES

Geodes (Figure 11) are a nice surprise. They're like those funny crepe-paper balls we used to find beside our plates at birthday parties—the ones that gradually unwound to reveal hidden presents inside. The word geode means earth-stone, and I'm not sure I can give you a sure-fire method for identifying one. But let's say you're walking along in what is supposed to be geode country and you find an old beat-up baseball that looks like it's turned to concrete. Check it out. Chances are it's a geode.

If it is, its interior can be filled with crystals in shades of green, blue or rose-brown. Sometimes the crystals are brilliantly clear and have no color at all. Though it's a rare occurrence, geodes occasionally contain pure gemstone material of great value. No two are alike, of course, since nature made them from whatever materials she had on hand at the time. They're different in different parts of the country too. The ones in central Oregon are called thunder eggs, and the Warm Springs Indians there have a legend that says these were the eggs of the great thunderbird. Warriors stole the eggs from their nests and hurled them at enemies across the mountain. Geodes are found in almost every state, although they are getting harder to find as time goes by.

JADE

Jade is the stone of heaven—that's what ancient Chinese scholars reported anyway. One of their legends says that in the beginning of the world, man was a helpless prey to all wild animals. He was doomed to extinction. But the storm god pitied him and forged jade axes out of the rainbow. Then he threw them down to earth for man to protect himself. This legend isn't hard to understand when you realize that jade comes in almost every color of the rainbow—not just the various shades of green we normally associate with it. It can be white, yellow, black, pink, gray or a mixture of colors.

Jade is still found today along the banks of streams and rivers or cuts and gullies where rivers once ran. Jade "pebbles" are fairly easy to locate, but as recently as 1970 a man and his wife uncovered a huge motherlode of jade high in the mountains of Wyoming. Photographs indicate they found chunks weighing several hundred pounds.

Many people want to polish, carve, mount or otherwise manipulate gemstones. If you want to do any of these things or have them done for you, the yellow pages will direct your energies. For example, an agate about the size of a healthy grapefruit was displayed on a bookshelf in my house for several years. I found Tom's Rock Shop listed in the Chicago phone book recently, and Tom sawed the stone into three parts for me—two halves and a smooth slice out of the middle. One part is mounted now in a small cradlelike wood piece. Mounts for large stones and jewelry findings for smaller ones can be purchased in rock shops. The Smithsonian Institution in Washington, D.C., and the Lizzadro Museum of Lapidary Art, Elmhurst, Illinois, are examples of places you can visit to see gem and nongem treatments.

Sources for Almost-Gems. Each state has its own unique rocks and minerals and its own state agency to disseminate information about them. Sometimes it comes from the office of the state geologist.

Sometimes it will be the Department of Conservation. For example, the Department of Natural and Economic Resources (Raleigh, North Carolina) publishes a free brochure called *North Carolina Gems.* "More than 300 different varieties of minerals and gems have been found here," it promises. It then lists a few to think about: emeralds, rubies, sapphires and garnet. It also provides information about sites where they can be found. The Department of Environmental Resources (Harrisburg, Pennsylvania) publishes an informative booklet called *Common Rocks and Minerals of Pennsylvania.* It lists and describes the state's rocks and minerals, museums, sites and pertinent reference manuals. Oregon's Highway Division publishes a booklet that pinpoints digging sites on a map and lists the state's rock clubs. So you see, these people *want* you to know about their rocks.

Check with the state Chamber of Commerce offices too and Tourist Information Centers. If they don't have the information, they'll know where it can be found.

Playing in Dirt, Sand and Clay

DIRT

One of the meanest tricks I ever played on anyone was one hot summer day when I was seven. I was playing "house" in the backyard and a loud-mouthed neighborhood kid kept hassling me and my dolls. I promised to give him a cookie if he'd leave me alone, and went off to the garden to mix up a batch of reddish dirt and water. When it was almost dry I sprinkled white sugary sand on top. The kid fell for it and swallowed a magnificent bite before he realized he'd been had. I don't remember how he retaliated, but it must not have been damaging because my memories of the event are 99 percent triumph with just a speck of guilt mixed in.

Dirt is wonderful, though you wouldn't think so by reading the dictionary. A foul or filthy substance it calls it—vile, mean or worthless. Well, what do *they* know? In some parts of the world, dirt is just the opposite of worthless. It's a precious commodity that's sought as eagerly as gemstones. On rocky, barren islands, soil (if we use that term interchangeably with dirt) has to be created out of rock. I don't know if you've noticed or not, but rock disintegrates *very* slowly. It's a centuries-long process and people go out and scoop it up by spoonfuls when it finally emerges.

Throughout most of the world, though, dirt is plentiful. And it's mostly free. It's been used in numerous and wondrous ways by people who had little else *but* dirt to work with. Houses made from a process called rammed earth were being built in America in the 1700s. And if there's any question about the durability of buildings made from the same ingredients as mud pies, let it be known that several of those old buildings are still in use today.

Another type of shelter, the adobe home of the southwestern United States, was at once beautiful and enduring. Adobe, a combination of sun-baked, claylike soil and straw, was made into bricks and then mortared with mud. The houses were in complete harmony with the earth. And no wonder. Their structure as well as everything in them, almost without exception, was organic.

In his book *New Mexico Village Arts* (Albuquerque, New Mexico: University of New Mexico Press, 1949, 1970) Ronald Dickey says: "Walls and floors of hand-plastered adobe gave gentle roundness and irregularities to the corners and the door and window openings. The villager could strengthen the tamped earth floor by soaking it with animal blood, which produced a tough springy surface, for blood is one of the strongest natural cohesives. The floor was covered with untanned bullhides and checkered carpets of hand-woven wool. All the woodwork, the doors, the ceiling, the furniture was of unpainted pine, bearing the patina of age and daily use."

Houses made from sod were used extensively when the prairies of this country were being settled. Chunks of sod cut from the earth were piled one on top of the other to make walls and were laid like shingles on top of rafters to make the roof. Sometimes less than a dollar's worth of material went into the making of a home, but it was a back-breaking endeavor. A man required the help of good neighbors in order to get the job done. Sod houses were wonderfully cool in the summer and warm in the winter, and no prairie wind could damage the thick dark walls. But the roof often leaked and the lady of the house was forced to cook with an umbrella held over the pot of beans. Occasionally a roof would fall in, necessitating a new roof and sometimes a new wife.

In addition to shelters, the earth's surface has provided pigments for decorating cooking pots, jars and human bodies. Pulverized and mixed with various wetting agents, it furnished shades of red, brown, black, white and, in rare cases, green or blue. Brick-red earth was used by Paiute Indians to ward off certain illnesses and to cure others. For instance, they found it a quick and effective cure for their infants' diaper rash.

Mud, dirt, earth, soil—whatever you call it—is so fascinating that I wish, I really wish, there was something palpable I could help you make from it. I don't think I want to recommend that you make mud pies. They taste terrible and leave grit in your mouth. Actually the only things I can think of (outside of the mud dolls made by ancient Chinese) are connected somehow to ceremonies. Ceremonies that are meaningful but neither practical nor portable. Like decorating your head with mud. A group of ladies in Swaziland take hundreds of tiny wisps of their hair and coat them with mud. When the mud dries they look like beautiful red chrysanthemums. But not many ladies I know would be willing to try it. In photographs, painted people dancing in the sun with red and yellow midsections, legs and noses look so beautiful that they make me want to paint my own body and dance around under the sky. But I can't really recommend that either, unless you happen to have friends who like to dance who also like muddy bodies.

SAND

Sand is another matter. Whether it actually is or not, it seems cleaner and is therefore less threatening to work with. Of course, it doesn't stick together like dirt or clay, but it comes in a generous variety of colors and textures and, as any child can tell you, it's unexcelled as a play medium. Sand, the more or less fine debris of rocks, is marvelous for scouring pots on camping trips, for sprinkling on streets to keep people and cars from slipping, and for filling up bags to hold back floodwaters. According to one rather cynical historian, it was also used by some grocers in colonial America. They added it to the sugar bin to make their product weigh more.

Sand has also been used as an art medium with great success. The Navaho Indians are noted for their sand paintings, which were created by sifting various colored sands into patterns directly on the

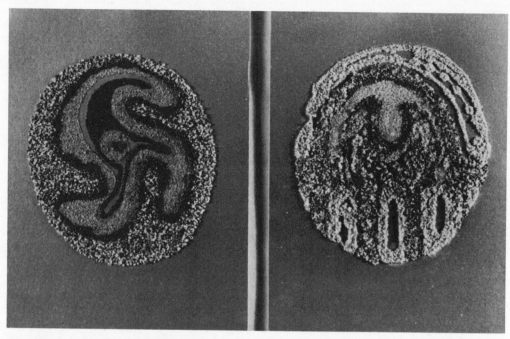

FIGURE 12 *Three different textured sands were used for these sand paintings. In addition, some of the sand was dyed. In some places the background of gold foil is allowed to show through. Sand can be "painted" on to any smooth surface that will take glue.*

surface of the earth. Because they were created as part of a religious ceremony, they were meant to be expendable. In other words, their destruction was an integral part of the painting. Because of the art world's interest in them, though, sand paintings are now being reproduced by contemporary Indian artists. They use the traditional sacred colors (red, black, blue, yellow and white) and symbols, but "paint" on a backing of plywood or other portable material.

SAND PAINTINGS *(Figure 12)*

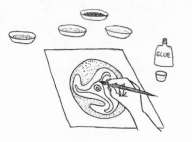

The paintings in Figure 12 make no attempt to duplicate Indian sand paintings. Instead, they illustrate that sand is fun to work with and can be used for any design that seems fitting to the artist at the time. It can be sifted onto sandpaper with a heavy backing, on plywood, or on any other sturdy backing material.

½ pound each of three different kinds of sand, two sheets of gold foil posterboard measuring 8″ x 10″, various dry ingredients for coloring, white glue, lacquer.

MATERIALS

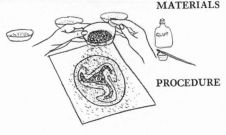

PROCEDURE

1. Draw a design on the posterboard with a pencil or felt-tipped pen.

2. "Paint" one section at a time with undiluted white glue, using the tip of the glue bottle or a brush (Figure 13a). To do fine work along lines, you may use a toothpick. While the glue is still wet, pour one color of sand over it and let it dry for several minutes (Figure 13b).

3. Pour off this sand and paint another section in the same way until you have filled in the whole painting (Figure 13c).

4. You may want to leave some areas free of sand and allow the color of the background to show through.

FIGURE 13
(a) *Painting glue to poster board*
(b) *Sprinkling one color of sand*
(c) *Pouring off sand after it has dried*

5. When all sand is dry (allow at least twenty-four hours to be sure), spray the painting with two coats of lacquer.

NOTES ON COLORING SAND: Sand can be colored by soaking it fifteen minutes in a solution of hot liquid dye. An easier procedure is to mix it with dry materials, such as dry tempera paints, colored chalks, paprika, ground cloves, cinnamon, cornmeal or dry mustard. In its natural state, sand ranges in color from pale cream to brown and, in some cases, black. It can be as fine as talcum or as rough as crushed gravel.

FIGURE 14 *The candle, left, was made by pushing a fist into wet sand to make a mold. The center one was formed with a cereal bowl. Legs were added to the one on the right by pushing the handle of a wooden spoon into the sand.*

The candles in Figure 14 are an indication of the versatility of sand as a molding medium. They were made by pouring wax into a depression made in a bucket of sand. Finger-sized candles can be made at the beach or campsite by employing the same technique. They will last just long enough for the evening's pleasure and will be totally consumed so they won't leave any litter.

SAND CANDLES *(Figure 14)*

To make candles at home, you will need a large bucket or box of sand, candlemaking supplies (wax, wicking, scent and color) and white glue. The sand should be about the same consistency as it would be if you were making sand castles at the beach—wet, but not sloppy-wet.

MATERIALS

1. Level the sand in the bucket with your hand. Pat it down so it is fairly compact. Press a shape

PROCEDURE

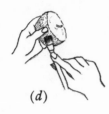

FIGURE 15

(a) *Pressing bowl into sand*
(b) *Wick centered over mold*
(c) *Pouring wax*
(d) *Brushing away loose sand*

into it by using your hand, a bowl, a glass or any other uncomplicated shape (Figure 15a).

2. Hang candle wick over center of mold (Figure 15b).

3. Using directions for candlemaking on pages 69–71, melt wax and add scent and coloring. Then pour wax into mold in sand, holding back a few ounces (Figure 15c). Be careful. Hot wax gets mean sometimes.

4. When completely cool (this takes approximately two hours), scoop candle from its bed and brush away the loose sand (Figure 15d). You will see that sand and wax have combined to give the look of an object carved from sandstone or dug from an ancient ruin. After the sand dries completely in the air, paint the surface with a solution of white glue, diluted one-to-one with water. This will keep additional sand from loosening later on. Only a thin coat is needed.

NOTE: Different effects can be obtained by using sands of different natural colors and textures. Also, you can vary the amount of sand that adheres to the candle. The cooler the wax, the less sand it will pick up. If the wax is smoking-hot, it will pick up about half an inch of sand.

Sources for Sand. Sand can be found on the beach, along river banks, in sand boxes and on kitchen floors (especially those located alongside the ocean). It can also be purchased from pet stores, lumber yards and foundries. It is very inexpensive. All the sand for the paintings in Figure 12 cost less than twenty-five cents. The bucket of sand cost less than a dollar.

CLAY

Like sand and dirt, clay is an integral part of the earth. It is plentiful and comes in a rich variety of colors and textures. Unlike commercial clay, which has all its impurities removed, native clay stands just as it is, with all its moles, warts, confusions and probably even a few internal injuries. As a result, making something with it is both exciting and risky. Not because the clay might hurt you, but because its rough, independent character won't always yield to the plans you have for it. Small bubbles or tiny bits of stone or twig can make a piece explode when it is being fired, or possibly interfere with the decorative process when lines are being drawn. But neither of these events is an insurmountable tragedy, and most people feel the risks involved add to the beauty of a piece of art (Figure 16).

The whole subject of clay and its uses in pottery and ceramics is too vast to cover in this book. And my knowledge is more playful than profound. So what I'll do is introduce you to natural clay, relate some of my own experiences and tell you how to have fun with it.

The Nature of Clay and How to Find It. Good places to look for clay are along banks that have

FIGURE 16 *A clay hanging made by Bernard Toale. It is made of clay dug from a roadbank in the Upper Peninsula of Michigan. Variously textured and organic, it looks like it might sprout some new parts.*

been cut away for construction or along stream and river beds. When you find something that looks suspiciously like clay, test it. Pick it up and roll it around in your palm. When it's wet it will stick together in a way that dirt or sand won't do. If you poke your finger into a mass of it, the impression will remain. Describing the color won't be of much help because, depending on the geography, it can be red, white, cream, black, gray or brown.

To dig it, take along a small shovel. One of those folding ones used in World War II for digging trenches is good. They have sharp triangular-shaped tips. They're sold today in camping supply shops. Dig clay in fairly small chunks so it will not be too heavy to carry. It can be placed in a number of small plastic garbage sacks.

If you want to try to pinpoint areas rich in natural clay before you leave home, check with your state geologist. A list can be obtained from the government (see page 19).

Before shaping natural clay, you need to free it of debris such as small rocks or twigs. Pick them out. If there seem to be enormous amounts of debris, spread the clay out on newspapers and let it dry. After it is dry, pick out the obvious waste matter and then pound the clay into small lumps. Place it in a crock or bucket and cover with water. Let it stand overnight and then pour the wet mixture through a coarse screen, kitchen sieve or colander. Stubborn lumps can be massaged through the screen with the hand. Be careful not to force twigs and pebbles through at the same time. The wet, screened mixture can be set aside in the bucket to dry to a workable consistency. (If you want to use it right away, remove several handfuls from the bucket and lay on newspapers to dry.) Roll and pat it into workable balls—about the size of an orange. The balls can be stored in plastic bags until needed.

Working with clay requires a consistency somewhat like that of bread dough. This means it will feel slightly spongy but not sticky. If it insists on sticking to your hands, it is too moist. Pat it out on newspapers for ten minutes or so. If it feels too dry, or the piece you are making starts getting minute cracks around the edges, spread out the clay and sprinkle water over it. Massage it in and knead it till it feels uniformly moist.

The last step before forming is to remove the unseen air bubbles. Take a ball of clay and throw it down hard, against a table. Pick it up, press it together and throw it down again. Do this several times. Some people call this "wedging."

Except for a very few places in the world, clay pieces are made permanent by baking them in kilns fired by gas or electricity. This is the least troublesome and most predictable method, but since most people don't have access to a kiln, it's good to know that pottery can be fired in an open fire. And, of course, many exciting pieces will not have to be fired at all. Historically, there are several methods of open firing, but the one used by Pueblo potters will serve as a guide. It's easy to duplicate the process. The pots to be fired were thoroughly dried, decorated, and then piled on a grate built a few inches off the ground. The grate was created from strips of metal laid over rocks, cans or old broken pots. After the pots were stacked, they were covered with chunks of metal or pot shards, and then a wood fire was built around and over them. Kindling was pushed under the grate and lit. The fire burned intensely for several hours and reached temperatures somewhere between 1,200 and 1,500 degrees Fahrenheit. For special effects, the fire was often smothered in cow dung or with heavy layers of grass. The pots were sometimes left in the ashes to cool, or they were checked and removed when the potter observed they were ready. Someone trying this method for the first time would do well to let the pots alone till they cooled, for sudden changes of temperature can cause cracks.

Because the temperature can't be perfectly controlled, all open-firing methods are chancy. But this isn't to say the effects are less beautiful or that they shouldn't be tried. Ladi Kwali, an artist from northern Nigeria, still uses the traditional method of open firing, and her spectacular pots are admired in museums and galleries all over the world.

FIGURE 17   *Top, Christmas tree ornaments. Center, three tiles. In the foreground, weed pots, candles, medallions and coins. All are of unfired roadbank clay. Some bits of grit and even sticks add to the personality of the pieces.*

Native artists decorated their pots in a variety of ways. Some pots were incised with crude tools of stone or bone. Additional clay was sometimes pinched onto the surface of the pots, or they were imprinted with whatever natural material was handy. Pigments often came from the surface of the earth and, depending on the location, were yellow, orange, white or brown. After being ground into a powder and mixed with water, they were painted directly onto the pot with brushes made of turkey-leg tendons or leaves of the yucca plant. Plant matter was also used for decorative color. Ladi Kwali often bastes her pots (while they're still hot) with a solution made from locust bean pods that have been soaked in water. This gives a rich mahogany-colored surface.

Even without firing, it's possible to make good presents from natural clay. You wouldn't want to drop them from a helicopter or pour hot soup into them, but with a minimum amount of care they will last for many years.

MATERIALS AND EQUIPMENT FOR MAKING THINGS FROM CLAY

A supply of clay (a medium-sized mixing bowlful will suffice), rolling pin, small sharp knife, a cloth to cover working surface, two strips of wood measuring ¼″ to ½″ thick and about a foot long, assorted objects to imprint the clay, electric drill with a 1/16″ bit, large darning needle.

1. Remove air bubbles from a ball of clay as described on page 40.

2. Place ball on cloth, centered between the two strips of wood (Figure 18a). Roll out flat and cut three tiles, 3" x 4" (Figure 18b). Incise design into surface by using the head end of the darning needle (Figure 18c). Turn tile over and score backside with several rows of incisions. This will help tile dry evenly.

3. Lay aside to dry. Allow ten days to two weeks to be sure they're moisture-free before you decorate them with color. When they're partially dry (leather-hard) any rough edges can be removed with the knife. When they're totally dry, surface can be smoothed with sandpaper. Small rolls of clay that might have balled up during the incision process can be removed at this time too. They will come off with the pressure of your fingernail.

4. See page 46 for decorating procedures.

5. When the tiles are decorated and are completed, drill a hole in each corner of the top of the tiles with a 1/16" bit and secure each tile to a sheet of plexiglass with thin wire drawn through holes in tiles and holes drilled in plexiglass. A bead keeps the wire in place.

Procedure is the same as for the preceding set of tiles. Roll out clay. Cut a design out of a piece of cardboard or paper and lay on slab. Cut around edge of the design with knife. Incise the pattern

3 TILES (*Figure 17, center*)

PROCEDURE

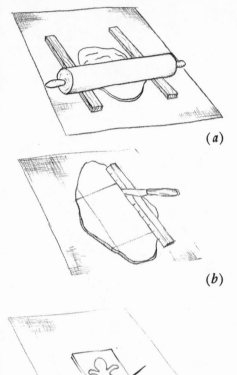

(*a*)

(*b*)

(*c*)

FIGURE 18
(*a*) *Rolling out the clay for tiles.*
(*b*) *Cutting it to shape.*
(*c*) *Drawing a design with head of needle.*

TREE DECORATIONS *(Figure 17, top)*
PROCEDURE

with head of darning needle. Poke a hole for hanging with the darning needle. As the clay dries, it shrinks, so check in 24 hours and if the hole seems small, enlarge it with needle. See page 46 for decorating procedures.

WEED POT *(Figure 17, left foreground)*

Prepare slab the same as for preceding projects. Using a free hand, roll up a section about three inches long and an inch to two inches wide. Keep the form very free. When you have a nice little roll, lay slivers of slab on top of the roll, pressing them down into the preceding ones as you go. Pinch on a dab of clay wherever you choose. When you're done playing with the form, push a hole down through the center for the weed. Let it dry. I didn't decorate this form at all, but sprayed it with a ceramic fixative called fix-it.

MEDALLIONS AND COINS *(Figure 17, right foreground)*

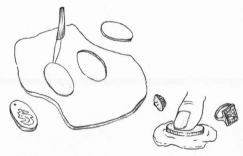

Roll out a slab of clay ½″ thick, or take a fingerful of clay and press it into your palm in the shape of a coin. Cut out the designs you wish, keeping the shapes fairly free (Figure 19). After they're cut, press a coin into the center of form for a design. An ornate dinner ring or a fancy button will also make a good design. Make hole for stringing. When dry, decorate according to procedures below. The coins can be strung on the heavy gold or silver crochet thread sold in fabric shops. They can be worn as jewelry or hung on a tree. I suppose they could even be mounted like rare coins.

FIGURE 19
Left, cutting out a coin-shaped piece of clay. Right, pressing a design into clay for medallions.

(1) Assortment of brushes. (2) Coloring matter—tempera paints, acrylics or ceramic dyes. Ceramic dyes can be purchased at an art supply shop. They are applied just like paint. (3) Tubes or jars of rub-on wax such as Metallic Luster Wax or Rub 'N' Buff. These waxes come in a large variety of colors—brass, pewter, gold, blue, etc. They can be applied as a solid color, or they can be applied and then partially rubbed off. The latter procedure gives a weathered, textured look that makes everything look like someone else had already loved it. It is a very nice finish for the rough nature of natural clay.

After objects are dry, they can be colored with any of the above media. Marking pens also work, but they tend to be absorbed very quickly. I used the same technique for all the above objects, painting with both acrylics and ceramic dyes. I painted one section at a time and wiped off some of the color before it dried because I wanted the pieces to have a weathered look. When this paint was dry, I rubbed the whole surface with wax. I rubbed it on sparingly at first, then wiped some of it away, gradually building up to the surface color I wanted. The wax gives an underplayed sheen and needs no final treatment other than a rub with a soft cloth.

3 WEED POTS (Figure 17, second row left)

Take a small handful of clay and shape it by throwing it against the table and patting and pushing it with your palms until you have a blocky, chunky figure that you like. Because they're not going to be fired, the pots need to be sturdy in order to survive. After the shape is formed, poke a hole down through the form with a darning needle or skewer. Make the hole deep enough to hold a weed stem and then check it occasionally as it dries. It will probably need to be enlarged several times as the clay shrinks. Turn the pot occasionally so the air can reach all of the sides. It will take ten days to two weeks for the pot to completely dry. See page 46 for decorating procedures.

4 REFILLABLE CANDLES (Figure 17, on pedestal)

Candles were made by the slab method (Figure 18). A slab was rolled out to ¼″ thickness and the cut end of a beef bone impressed on its surface (Figure 20). Strips were then cut from the slab varying from 1″ to 3″ wide and 3″ long. They were rolled into a cylinder and the ends overlapped ½″. Ends were then carefully pressed together. After they were dried and decorated, they were filled with candle wax. See pages 69–71 for complete candlemaking instructions.

DECORATING
WEED POTS AND CANDLES
(Figure 17)

These figures were coated with a product called Boss Gloss, a liquid medium that can be applied directly to raw clay after it has dried. It gives the rich glossy look of a glaze, but the process doesn't require any heat. The instructions accompany the product, but here is a brief summary of the way it works. Two solutions are mixed together when you are ready to begin work. They consist of a curing agent and a coloring agent in a syrupy form. When the two are mixed, the liquid is then brushed or poured onto the object and allowed to dry. Drying is a long process. Depending on the object's size, etc., drying can take as long as two weeks, although it can be handled during the drying process. Boss Gloss is available from major craft stores and from the mail-order catalog of the J. C. Penney Company.

What I've told you here is no more than a fleeting introduction to the subject of clay. It's very possible you will want to expand your experience. Helpful books are listed in the Books and Other Printed Sources of Information and Enjoyment, under Clay.

FIGURE 20 *Left, a section of soup bone pressed into clay to make textured design. Right, a finished candle ready to have the wax poured into it.*

EARTH-BORN THINGS

Wild Weeds, Pods and Mushrooms

I HAVE unlimited affection for weeds. For violent purple thistles protecting abandoned buildings, for mullein and teasel—even for dandelions. And for wild barley that waves its foxy tail along the edges of furrowed land. These so-called useless, pernicious plants have cornered my affection because they represent the invincibility of nature. Set down in any hard scrabble soil (or even some slender rocky vein), they manage to laugh and carry on when finer, more highly bred plants falter and die.

After centuries of being kicked aside, rooted out or ignored, many weeds have suddenly gained respectability and even a certain amount of gran-

deur. Gift shops and craft and plant stores do a
thriving business in the stems, pods and branches
of weeds that for the most part are free for the
finder. One of the handsomest weeds in my collection, for instance, was pulled from a strip of dirt
beside the parking lot of my grocery store. It's
sturdy and tough, with a silver stem that ends in a
clutch of outspread arms (Figure 21).

Autumn is the best time to go looking for weeds
or, for that matter, for fallen branches, sprays,
pods, seed cases and cones. A few nights of frosty
weather will strip away summer foliage and lay
bare the intricate framework of a plant's skeleton.
Milkweed plants display a long stem with taste-
fully spaced pods. When fireweed loses its bright
blossoms, rows of ladylike fingers curl around
empty spaces the shape of teacups. Whole fields
of goldenrod can be found with their flowers replaced by one single fat oval pod. This pod is actually a gall, the handiwork of a worm. Or an in-
sect—I can never remember which.

GATHERING

For tools you'll need just your mind, body and a
pocket knife—though it wouldn't hurt to take
along a cheerful companion to share the pleasures
of weed gathering. It's no use telling you where
to look because each section of the country has its
own exciting weeds. But you may not know about

FIGURE 21   *Parking-lot weeds in a pot made by Bernard Toale.*

railroad rights-of-way. These strips of land are prime and juicy sources for unusual weeds. They were fenced off years ago and have never been plowed or paved. Or even grazed by animals. So unless chemical weed killers have gradually discouraged good weeds to death, these ribbons of land will be a source of pleasure for any serious weed gatherer. The same conditions exist in and around old cemeteries too. And this brings up the point that weeds should never be gathered indiscriminately. We should take only what will be put to good use and enjoyed. Keep in mind that in some areas, particularly state and national parks, it is illegal to pick *any* kind of plant. It's a good idea to check before doing any gathering.

CARE AND HANDLING

Shake off any hardy bugs before taking plants inside. Remove dirt and roots and lay weeds out on newspapers to dry. Give them plenty of space and turn them occasionally. Many of them will already be dry and you can display them in whatever container you wish to use. After I've used them for a while, I tie them in loose bundles and hang them from the attic ceiling. Weeds will profit from being sprayed with several coats of a fixative. I have used one called fix-it. Hair spray will do the trick too—five or six coats. No fixative will keep stray seeds under control forever, but this doesn't

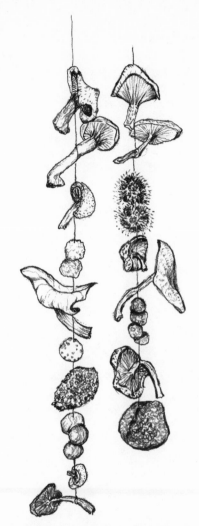

seem to matter. It's very nice to look up from a book in the middle of February to see a milkweed seed on its way across the living room.

Any stalks that are weak can be reinforced with florist's wire or a piece of wire from the hardware store. Cut the wire the length of the stem and wrap the two together with colored yarns. Or use a flat florist's tape. It is sold by the yard and is usually green.

Weeds can be colored. Lay them out on newspapers and spray with shoe dyes. These dyes come in small cans in a wide range of colors. They leave a very faint sheen that doesn't detract from the natural appearance of the dried material. Spray as many coats as needed to obtain the desired color. This spray also acts as a fixing agent.

SUGGESTIONS FOR USE

A whole fat tumbleweed, the kind that blows across the highway in the western states, looks beautiful suspended from a ceiling. It can obscure a light fixture and make lace patterns on the walls and floor. Even though they're larger than pumpkins, they're very lightweight. If you're going to give one away, attach a note that tells where it came from. You might want to mention that every autumn these plants deliberately detach themselves from their mother roots and take off on lonesome journeys.

FIGURE 22 *Galls, mushrooms, chestnut pods and fungus are strung on yarn and dry in a variety of twisted shapes. These two strings are part of a large group that almost fills a doorway in the author's home.*

Pods, leaves and galls can be removed from their stalks and strung on yarn. I hang them in groups from a fallen branch and suspend them in open spaces. They are mixed with nuts, thistle tops and mushrooms (Figure 22).

Tiny weeds can be given importance by featuring each one in a small container (Figure 23) or on a length of velvet ribbon. Pull top of ribbon through a curtain ring and glue in place. I use a glue called Liquid Cloth. Turn up and hem at bottom and glue in place. Place drops of glue on several spots of the foliage and hold in place a few moments. Allow to dry thoroughly before hanging (Figure 24).

LOOKING SEEDS

Seeds and Plants for Looking, Wearing and Eating

A writer once described seeds as being exquisitely designed instruction capsules for an orderly arrangement of the elements. But they seem more like plain old magic to me. Prickled, speckled, glossy, dry, round or flat, they come in every size from dust motes to coconuts. And each resourceful seed not only packs its own lunch but also comes with the standard equipment it needs to travel around the country. The seeds of the maple, for instance, sprout translucent red wings. Flat brown seeds of the milkweed are attached to lighter-than-air white feathers that lift them through space. And many unwinged models have bodies coated with

FIGURE 23   *Vials 3 inches high are filled with black, red and white sand. Honesty and baby's breath form a white background for tiny red dried flowers.*

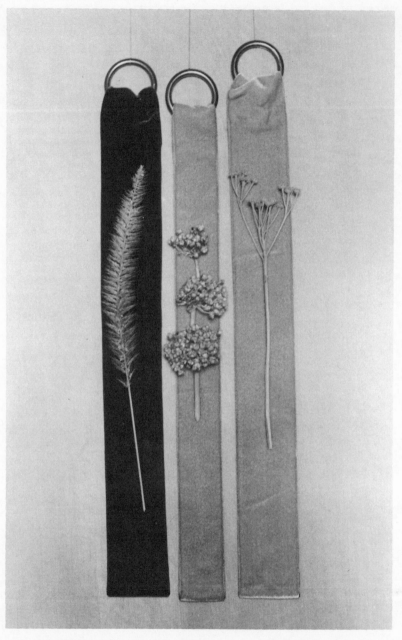

FIGURE 24 *Roadside grasses and seeded tops of an onion plant in their natural colors are glued to brown, orange and gold lengths of velvet ribbon.*

FIGURE 25 *Milkweed seeds are floating inside a Mexican tin and glass lantern. They are silvery white with an occasional flat brown seed pod.*

prickles and spines so they can grab a ride on the fur of four-footed animals. Their infinite variety and beauty make them such fascinating pieces of natural art that they can be displayed as though they were national treasures (Figure 25).

Backyard gardens, fields and marshes are free sources of handsome seeds. The tops of onion, garlic and chive are beautiful. So are the seeds and pods from the poppy, thistle, peony and honesty plants. Seed pods from trees lie on the ground and are free for the taking—maple, locust, catalpa, chestnut, etc. Unusual or exotic seeds can be purchased from gift shops or from mail-order sources listed in the Sources of Supplies and Information.

WEARING SEEDS

Outside of having seeds around to remind you of their magic, I can't think of anything nicer than putting them into decorations for bodies (Figure 26). Their natural colors can be used, or the pale ordinary ones can be dyed bright colors. Since their shapes and sizes vary, they can be mixed into a mad variety of necklaces and bracelets. Supermarkets and seed stores sell beans that are red and purple and white and black. Or deep brown with one white eye. Next to them are yellow and green peas, olive green lentils, and rich dark coffee beans.

FIGURE 26 *Necklace, left, is made of Swedish yellow peas, cantaloupe and dyed squash seeds. The center one is made of chestnuts strung on brown goatskin lacing. The small seeds at the bottom are black beans. Right-hand necklace is clove mixed with black peppercorns and a few bright yellow glass beads.*

MATERIALS AND TECHNIQUES

1. There are half a dozen different kinds of bead threads available for stringing seeds. They vary from very fine nylon to the kind of nylon used by fishermen. You can also buy a fine bead wire. Elasticized thread is good for chokers and bracelets. Clasps may come from discarded necklaces, though many necklaces are made long enough so no clasp is needed.

2. Seeds and beans are soaked overnight to make them soft enough for stringing. Nuts or large seeds like the apricot must be drilled.

3. If you plan to dye seeds, skip the soaking part and place them directly in the dye while it is still very hot. In the morning, rinse until the water runs absolutely clear. Seeds are strung while still damp, but there's no need to hurry. It takes many hours for them to harden again. Tintex and Rit are the dyes I've used.

4. Add scent to necklaces by using soaking water to which a few drops of your favorite perfume have been added. Whole cloves and cinnamon sticks add a delicious scent when incorporated into a necklace. Their scent will still be apparent months later.

5. Leather lacing may be used as part of the design of a necklace. It is available from craft shops and leather supplies. Ask for lacing rather than thong. Thong is much heavier.

6. Finished necklaces should be sprayed with several coats of lacquer. It gives a waxlike sheen.

In the case of dyed seeds, it keeps any leftover dye from staining your neck.

You may use Figure 26 as a starting point for ideas for body ornaments and proceed from there with your own ideas. The following is a partial list of natural materials that can be used.

Seeds and Nuts

whole white pepper	butternut squash
whole black pepper	acorn squash
mustard	castor beans
cantaloupe	cedar berries
pumpkin	acorns
watermelon	sliced walnuts
honeydew melon	

Beans and Peas

azuki	navy
fava	purple pod
black	pinto
kidney	black-eyed peas
mung	Swedish yellow peas
soy	lentils

Others

pits from peaches, apricots, cherries, prunes, etc.

EATING SEEDS

Many seeds are not only delicious but also come packed with a rich variety of nutrients. Sunflower seeds, for instance, contain vitamin B, calcium and iron. Protein is a bonus—a half cup contains twelve grams. Compare that to a doughnut, which contains only two grams, or a piece of fudge, which has none at all. Instead of throwing away the seeds of such vegetables as butternut squash, save and toast them for a snack food.

Some examples of seeds that can be eaten are sunflower, pumpkin, butternut squash and sesame seeds. Soy beans can also be toasted and are delicious. Soak them overnight, simmer for one hour, pat dry on a paper towel and then toast. I'm sure other seeds can be treated in this fashion, but these are the only ones I've actually tried myself. Following is a recipe for a tasty sauce to stir into the seeds before putting them in the oven.

For four cups of seeds, mix together 4 tablespoons salad oil or melted butter, 2 tablespoons Worcestershire sauce, 1 tablespoon garlic salt, ½ cup grated Parmesan cheese and 1 tablespoon salt-flavored butter. Place seeds in large flat pan, pour mixture over all and stir well. Place in oven for two hours at 325 degrees Fahrenheit. Stir at half-hour intervals.

The toasted seeds can be packaged in clear plastic wrap and labeled if you're going to give them away—or even if you're not. If you grow your own pumpkins, you might like to know that a new variety has been developed with hull-less seeds. They are perfect for toasting.

SEEDS TO SPROUT BEFORE EATING

Sprouts have only recently been discovered by Americans, but they have been a staple food in Oriental countries for hundreds of years. They're crunchy and delicious and contain miraculous amounts of protein and vitamins—more nutrients, in fact, than any other vegetable. In the sprouting process, which is easy to carry out, all the seed's inherent power and glory are allowed to escape and be put to use. By you. Once outside its husk, the sprout begins to grow with amazing speed. It's fun to watch it happen even if you don't want to have sprouts for lunch. They can grow as much as an inch a day, and (depending on the seed or bean) will be ready to eat in three to four days. The easiest seeds to sprout are the tiny earth-green mung beans. Next are lentils. Others to try are soybeans, corn, dry peas, garbanzos, fava beans and the seeds of sunflower and pumpkin. The seeds of almost any grain can be sprouted too—wheat, alfalfa, oats, barley, buckwheat and rye. Each has its own distinct flavor.

There are a variety of methods for sprouting, including the use of sprouting kits, but the one I describe here for mung beans has been quite successful for me and is suitable for other beans and grains as well. It's an easy way to begin.

SPROUTING MUNG BEANS

PROCEDURE

1. Wash ½ cup mung beans and let soak overnight in water at room temperature.

2. In the morning, pour off soak-water, rinse, and place two sheets of paper toweling in the bottom of an opaque mixing bowl. A stainless-steel bowl will do too. The idea is to keep the beans in the dark, and moist, but not wet. Place drained beans in bowl, cover with one sheet of dampened paper toweling, and cover bowl with a plate. Keep at room temperature (anywhere from 65 to 75 degrees Fahrenheit.

3. Rinse three times a day and change paper toweling each time. The toweling will soak up extraneous moisture. Repeat each day until sprouts are grown. Mung beans will be ready in three to four days. Beans with larger, harder kernels will take longer. Generally, the sprouts are considered mature when they are as long as the bean.

4. Grains are treated in the same fashion except that they don't have to be presoaked, and they take less time to sprout. Alfalfa is a good grain to start with. The sprouts are thin and threadlike. For variety occasionally mix grains in with larger seeds.

5. To store sprouts, drain thoroughly and place in refrigerator. They keep for a week and will also freeze well.

Suggestions for Use. Sprouts are delicious when added to salads, especially winter salads. They can also add dash to soups, omelets and casseroles. When I want to serve them as a vegetable (perhaps along with eggs or rice), I put 2 tablespoons oil in a skillet and add 2 tablespoons chopped onions. They are stirred until golden, then a cup of sprouts is added and stirred. Three to five minutes is plenty of cooking time. At the last minute I add 1 tablespoon soy sauce.

To give sprouts away, I make up a batch and put it in a pretty transparent package. I include the directions for sprouting and a pound of the dry beans too.

Sources. Use only untreated seeds for sprouting. They are available in a number of places—health food stores, granaries and some food stores. Walnut Acres, Penns Creek, Pennsylvania 17862, is a mail-order source for a large variety of sprouting seeds. They also carry Beale's Famous Seed Sprouter, which comes with a selection of seeds and full instructions for sprouting. It makes sprouting a bit easier than the mixing-bowl method.

Plants to Eat, Dry, Look at, Sprout and Smell

The pioneers and Indians and nearly everyone else who wanted to live through a long, cold winter had to find a way to dry and store their harvest. Thanks to modern food processing and refrigeration, we don't have to be concerned with that today. But it is fun to experiment with some of the food-preservation techniques used by our ancestors. In addition, having strings or piles of brightly colored fruits and vegetables hanging around the kitchen provides a nice exhibit of changing color and form.

Nearly any fruit or vegetable can be dried, though some are better suited for this process than others. Some of the foods I'm familiar with are: all kinds of squash, parsnips, carrots and corn kernels. Cabbage leaves, spinach, kale, green and red peppers, lettuce leaves, and all beans and peas. Peaches, apples, apricots, pineapples and cranberries are the fruits I've tried. Of course, any herb can be dried too—basil, parsley, thyme, etc.

THE DRYING PROCESS

1. Choose the most perfect specimens you can find; wash and open them to the air. For example, fruit should be peeled and cored and all imperfections removed. It is then cut so no section is over a half inch thick.

2. Spread slices on a large cloth-covered screen or a tray. Cover with cheesecloth to keep away bugs. Keep cheesecloth from resting directly on the produce by raising it at the corners with rocks or blocks of wood. Keep produce dry and turn occasionally. Check for any imperfect pieces that might begin to rot. Throw them out.

3. Leaves, pepper slices, cranberries and small bunches of herbs can all be strung with a needle on nylon thread. Slice peppers into inch-wide strips. Leaves should be left whole unless they're

exceptionally large and heavy. Strings should be hung inside to dry, unless you know a way to keep outdoor bugs away.

4. Drying times vary—none is less than two weeks. You'll have to use your judgment about whether or not all moisture has left the produce. When you think it's dry, package it in plastic bags and secure top of bag with rubber band. If moisture begins to collect, it means it's not quite dry. Give it some more time and then package.

5. To use, soak in water-to-cover until produce softens.

DRIED FRUITS AS DECORATION

One of the most intriguing pieces of sculpture I've ever seen was made from a grapefruit. An artist had peeled the whole fruit, carefully keeping the rind intact. He set the peeling down on a shelf, letting it assume its natural spherical shape, and the air in the room took over from there. It dried in such an interesting form that he began making these "sculptures" for friends every time he had grapefruit for breakfast. He admits he ate a lot more grapefruit than usual for several weeks.

A surprising number of fruits can be air-dried and then used in decorative arrangements with other plant materials. They can certainly make solo appearances without any apology too (Figure 27). Lemons, limes, pomegranates, cumquats, grape-

FIGURE 27 *Pomegranate, orange, lemon and grapefruit dried to rich deep colors.*

fruits, tangelos, oranges and tangerines are the ones I've tried successfully. An artichoke dries beautifully too, as do the leaves of cabbage, beets and horseradish.

PROCEDURE

1. Select luscious, proud-looking fruits. The drying process won't make a piece of fruit look any healthier than it did in the market.

2. Using an ordinary needle, prick fruit close to the stem end and at the opposite end.

3. Set it down any place in the house where it won't get stepped on, rained on, or thrown in the garbage. I like to keep it in sight because it undergoes several color changes and gives off a nice fragrance. The top of the refrigerator, a window sill or sunny shelf will do. Turn it occasionally so it doesn't flatten on one side—you want it to be (at least partially) round.

4. Most fruit darkens as it dries. Grapefruit changes to the color of expensive pigskin gloves. The pomegranate becomes an exotic, almost-purple red. Lemons go deep gold, and oranges develop a rich brown hue. Fruits may soften initially but will go past this stage to become almost rockhard.

5. Drying time depends on the air temperature, humidity, etc., but I would say that it takes at least a month for all the moisture to leave the fruit. Then it becomes as light as a sheet of paper. Nothing further needs to be done to preserve it,

unless you want to rub it with clear paste wax for sheen.

TRANSFORMING EDIBLES TO LOOKABLES

Hardly anybody I know eats turnips any more. Or parsnips either. They seem to have become the pale, poor relatives of the produce department. But they will sprout into handsome foliage plants if you treat them right. So will carrots, beets, radishes and sweet potatoes. To get the transformation started, cut the top (the leaf end) off and place the other end in a container of water. Set aside in a mildly dark place and watch to see that the water level remains constant. In time, threadlike roots will begin to appear at the base—a matter of ten days to two weeks. When roots begin to really flourish, move it to a sunny spot. The plant can be kept in the original container of water or it can be transplanted into potting soil. The resulting greenery varies with the type of plant, but whatever it is, it will be pretty and green.

The discarded top of a pineapple will also grow and develop new leaves if you place it in a flat bowl filled with pebbles and water. Wiggle the pineapple top into a stable position among the pebbles and be sure that at least the bottom inch of the top is submerged at all times. It needs no direct sunlight.

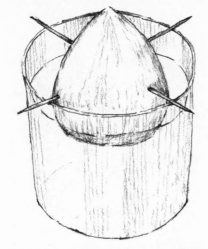

FIGURE 28 *Avocado seed with its flat bottom in water. Some day a sprout will burst out of the pointed end and it can be potted in soil.*

Avocado and mango seeds are sprouted by suspending the seeds in a container of water. Press toothpicks into seed at four places around its middle, pointed end up. Hang in a water-filled glass. Keep water level constant. It should reach halfway up the seed (Figure 28). When the sprout appears, pot it in soil. The sprouting time varies so much that it isn't possible to tell you when to expect results. One of my avocados waited nine months to sprout. Another got the job done in three weeks. Seeds can be potted directly into soil too. Place in pot, pointed end up. Cover with an inch of soil. Keep out of direct sunlight until a good-sized sprout appears and then move it to a sunny spot to carry on.

Using Plants and Other Natural Forms as Candle Molds

In the fall when squash, gourds and pumpkins are in season, they can be gathered and used as molds for candlemaking. The object is not only to form a shape but also to impress organic designs onto the skin of the candle itself. When the wax cools and the vegetable mold is removed, membranes and seeds will have left a tattoo of rivulets, indentations and gouges (Figure 29).

CANDLEMAKING

Ordinary kitchen paraffin can be used in the production of candles, but it should be hardened with a chemical called stearic acid, available at drug stores and most craft supply outlets. Add it to melted wax in the proportion of 2 tablespoons to 3 pounds of wax. When buying regular candle wax, choose the kind that melts at a temperature ranging from 140 to 150 degrees Fahrenheit.

Wax is extremely flammable, so melt it over water in a double boiler. A large coffee can can also be used, providing it is set in a pan of water. To give an idea of volume, a large squash will hold 2 pounds of wax. A small gourd requires only ¼ pound.

Color and scent are added after wax has melted. Color can come from old broken crayons (and, of course, new ones) or from any of the coloring compounds sold for that purpose. In place of store-bought scents you can try cinnamon, cloves and vanilla from the kitchen cupboard.

Some people use kitchen string for wicks, but it has disappointed me so many times I never use it now. Wicking is very inexpensive and comes in a variety of dimensions and twists. The kind with a wire center is nice for fragile molds such as the green pepper.

To prepare mold for use, cut off the vegetable top and scoop out pulpy matter, seeds and membranes. Leave enough inside, though, to add a nice design to your candle. Place wick over center of mold by tying it to a skewer, pencil or toothpick (Figure 30). It should have some kind of weight

FIGURE 29 *Large candle, left, is cinnamon color. The organic material captured in the wax is gold and pale brown. It was made in a pumpkin. The smaller candle, made in a green pepper, is dark red.*

FIGURE 30 *Pumpkin with insides removed, ready to receive melted wax.*

on it so it will hang straight. In the case of large molds such as pumpkin or squash, I make a tiny hole at the bottom of the squash and poke the wick into it. I pour in a small amount of wax and let it harden, and then add the rest of the wax a bit at a time until about an inch has hardened. The rest of the wax can then be added all at once. Hold back several ounces of wax. As wax cools it shrinks, and a depression will form around the wick. As a skin forms on the top, prick it close to the wick and add more wax. It will take two or possibly three fillings before the candle cools and remains level.

When cool, cut away vegetable mold. In the case of hard-skinned squash, you may have to use a coping saw. Oranges and such can just be peeled, as can peppers. Strip away any unwanted membranes, seeds, etc. The ones you leave behind will whiten and look beautiful. Flatten bottom of candle by heating an electric skillet to the lowest temperature. Place candle in skillet and rotate it until it has a flattened bottom and sits up nice and straight.

The plants I've used as molds are: green and red peppers, gourds of all sizes and shapes, butternut, turban and acorn squash, pumpkins, oranges, grapefruit, lemons and eggplants.

Ordinary barn straw, the stem of such grains as wheat, rye, oats and barley, was used as an art medium by nineteenth-century artists in Mexico and New Mexico. They split the stems lengthwise, cut them to length, and pressed them into beds of black pitch. These remarkable mosaics decorated closet doors, boxes, candlesticks and picture frames. No effort was made to hide the pitch, since it was meant to be part of the total effect. A straw star, for instance, seemed to shine in a black sky.

Country folk in rural England once used straw for art purposes too. They wove enormously complicated mobiles and figures from grain stalks, and hung them from ceilings and doorways. Some of them functioned as decorative items, others as good-luck charms in the hope of a plentiful harvest. Large numbers of European craftsmen also adapted straw for craft purposes. The Lithuanians were especially adept at weaving with straw, and the design of the ornaments they handed down from one generation to the next are exquisite (Figure 31).

It's easy to see how a person with a creative soul might be attracted to straw. Its silky yellow sheen and slender stalk invite the touch. The stems of wheat, rye, oats and barley are all called straw, but for craft purposes rye, wheat and oats are the best

Golden Straw for Golden Ornaments

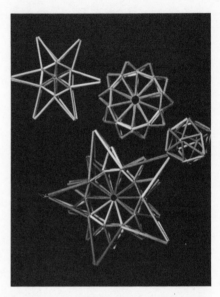

FIGURE 31 *Lithuanian ornaments made by Pauline Vaitaitis from natural straw. The artist starts out with one triangular group of straws threaded on cotton crochet thread. New groups of triangles are added to the original until a whole structure is formed. They gleam when the light strikes them.*

materials to work with, with rye at the top of the list.

Sources for Straw. Straw can be gathered from the neighboring countryside. One large armful will be enough for a considerable number of projects, and this much can probably be had for the asking. If you do your "harvesting" just as the seed heads are beginning to form in late summer, the seeds will remain intact inside their cases. But this is only important if you want to display the material as full stalks of grain. Otherwise, any time before a heavy freeze will be fine. As a matter of fact, it may be easier to get grain late in the season—as late as November. If it's still in the field, it probably means the farmer has decided not to harvest it and will be happy to have you carry away several armfuls. Don't worry if the grain has fallen over. It's still usable.

County and state agricultural fairs are an excellent source for whole sheaves of grain. Many farmers display their grain and then throw it away afterward. They can be contacted by consulting the identification tags on the displays. Commercial sources for grains are florists' shops and plant stores. Many gift shops sell them, but straw bought like this will prove to be too expensive to cut up for craft purposes. So try to find some in the field, unless you only want to make a very few things.

FIGURE 32 *Straw roping is easy to make. Large groups can be hung together to make Christmas swags.*

PREPARATION

Grain stalks are laid out to dry on newspapers—either outdoors or inside, as long as they're kept dry. Turn them occasionally to prevent mold. Drying takes about two weeks. Those dried in the shade (or in the dark) will be lighter in color than those that receive light. When dry, tie in bunches and hang from rafters. Or spread between sheets of tissues in boxes. They will keep for many years.

To prepare stalks for use, cut away tough ends (and seed cases if you're not going to use them). Strip away leaves and so on with fingernail and soak stalks for half an hour to make them pliable. They can be kept damp in plastic bags while you work with them. If you want to flatten straw, split it with your nail while damp and press with a cool iron.

DECORATIVE STRAW ROPING
MATERIALS

Batch of straw, needle, spool of strong nylon thread, scissors.

PROCEDURE

Straw for roping does not need to be soaked first. Cut a length of thread 40″ long. Cut about a mixing-bowlful of straw into lengths of 1″ and 2″. Make first cluster by stringing eight straws together, through the center of straws (Figure 32). Push together on thread. String one length of straw lengthwise, running the thread through the hollow stem, and push back against cluster. Place one of these dividers between each cluster and continue to string until you reach the end. Make as many lengths as you wish and tie them together. You can make your lengths longer if you like, but they sometimes get tangled if they are too long.

STRAW WREATH (Figure 33)
MATERIALS

1. A wire wreath-frame available from plant, craft and florist shops. They sell in sizes ranging from 10″ to 20″ and cost from 30 cents to 55 cents each.
2. A grocery-sackful of straw. It can be the ends and scrappy pieces discarded when you are making things that require perfect straws.
3. Decorative material such as cones or nuts or dry flowers.
4. Spool of yellow thread (to blend with straw).
5. Kitchen twine.
6. White glue.
7. Lacquer.

PROCEDURE

Place wreath frame on table and lay one handful of dampened straw over it, following the shape of the frame. Continue to lay on handfuls of straw and wrap kitchen twine loosely around it as you go to keep it in place as you continue to fill in wreath. Keep the back of the wreath flat so it will hang nicely against a wall. When frame is covered and tied temporarily into shape, lay in a basin filled with water to which white glue has been added—one cup to each gallon of water. Weight down and soak wreath for fifteen minutes. Remove,

FIGURE 33 *Glistening golden straw is laid over a 10-inch wreath frame. It is decorated with chestnuts and some Wisconsin roadside weeds in their natural brown hues.*

drain and lay out on papers to dry. When dry, clip away any unruly strands of straw, wrap where needed with matching yellow thread, and cut away the temporary twine. Decorate by tying dried flowers, pods or nuts onto frame. Spray finished wreath with four thin coats of lacquer.

Colored paper, gold notary seals, Liquid Cloth (an adhesive available in variety stores and hardware stores), felt-tipped markers, lengths of straws.

STRAW FIGURES (Figure 34)
MATERIALS AND EQUIPMENT

PROCEDURE

BIRD: Using the simple design in Figure 34 as a guide, cut a body from colored paper. This figure is 3 ″ across and 1½″ high. Draw a beak, eye, feathers, etc., with marker on cutout figure. Flatten three damp straws with your hands and glue across back of bird. Use slivers of four flattened straws for wings and topknot and glue in place. Press under weight for ten minutes. Glue notary seal behind bird's head.

MAN AND WOMAN: Using Figure 34 as a guide, cut a body and head from colored paper. Using markers, draw faces and clothing on paper figures. Cut seven straws 6″ long for each body. Tie in a bunch to make a neck, leaving about 1½″ above neckline. Fan out straws below neck and flatten with hands. Glue head and body to straws while holding them out flat. Cover for ten minutes with a heavy book to be sure they dry flat. Glue notary seals behind heads.

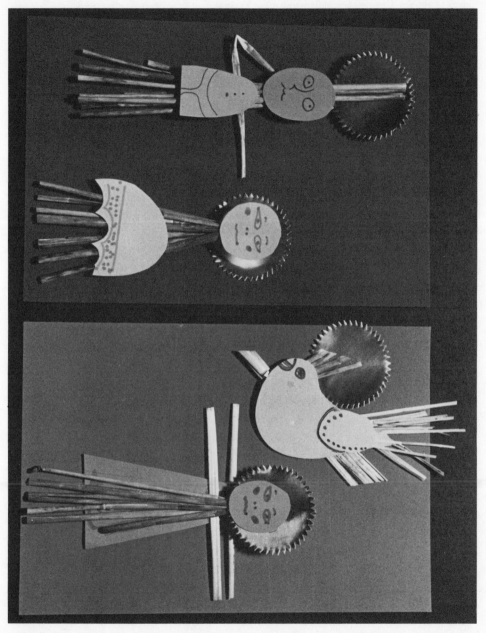

FIGURE 34 *Straw and colored paper made these figures, which are meant to be hung as ornaments. Gold notary seals are the halos. They are approximately 4 inches high.*

A lot of people believe that corn, rather than the eagle, should be the symbol of the United States. After spending considerable time with it recently, I'm ready to agree. This isn't meant to disparage the eagle, an elegant bird indeed. But corn has played a supporting role to the superstars of nature for so many centuries that I can understand why corn people want to honor it. Maybe if it had been able to fly or lay an occasional egg, it would have received more adulation over the years.

It is known for certain that corn grew in the Americas for at least a thousand years before Columbus ever set sail. By that time, in fact, two or three hundred different varieties had already been developed. In addition to the white and yellow kernels we know today, people grew blue, pink, purple, black, red and even variegated varieties. According to scientists from the Smithsonian Institution, even the tassels, leaves, silk and cobs were grown in a number of colors. Some were the result of a search for a particular flavor or texture, while others were obviously grown simply because someone wanted his corn to be red or pink or purple. It was, in fact, the job of certain men to propagate seeds for specific colors year after year.

Corn was invaluable as a food crop, rich in important nutrients and adaptable to almost any situ-

Amazing Corn

ation. Because it was easy to store and transport, it sustained whole populations through long winter months. Apparently every part of the plant was used—the stalk, shucks, kernels, silk and even smut —a fungus disease that sometimes attacks corn. Because it played such an important part in their lives, corn was the basis of many religious ceremonies. The Seneca Indians held marathon dances each year as a way of offering thanks to the Great Spirit for the gift of this grain. The Iroquois wove elaborate masks from shucks in the belief that they provided the gift of prophecy. Some groups believed that man and woman were created from corn. Others assumed this plant came to them as a miracle— that it was a gift straight from the gods. They may have been right. Scientists today still engage in friendly but so far unsolved arguments about its origin. One fact is certain, though: neither the Pilgrims nor the settlers at Jamestown would have survived their first year in America without this plant. When their descendants and other groups moved away from the coast and began to settle inland, they took corn seeds with them. Again it became an almost indispensable item. In addition to its use as table food, pioneers fed the green stalks and kernels to horses, pigs, chickens and cows. They burned the cobs for fuel, braided the husks into sun bonnets, sandals, chair seats and mats for the floor. The husks were split and woven into roping to make bed supports and collars for

FIGURE 35   *A cob with a painted face forms the body of the lady on the left. Her skirt is calico. The doll to the right is made entirely of corn shucks, except for the wisp of a hat made from cob. The cornstalk fiddle, center, has a classic beauty even though its tone is unmusical.*

mules and horses. Homemade mattresses were filled with the noisy, scratchy husks. And pipes made from cobs are still being marketed today. Small wonder that corn developed a few magical properties too. Like curing warts. All one had to do, according to folklorists who study these things, was to throw a kernel (one for each wart) over his left shoulder into a river or bayou.

In a remarkable display of good humor and invention, the pioneer woman began to make dolls from both the cobs and shucks of corn (Figure 35). After soaking the shucks to make them pliable, she bent and twisted them into figures of men and women, right down to arms, hands and even aprons and pants. Sometimes she gave them corn-silk hair. She painted rosy, healthy faces on cobs and covered the figures with handmade dresses, bonnets and aprons. I suspect the cob doll was actually played with, while the one made from husks may have been a more decorative item.

Musical instruments made from corn stalks are one of the best examples I know of the American pioneer's ability to make something out of nothing. Fifes, whistles and fiddles all emerged from the corn patch. None of them could have played along with the Boston Pops, but for a man or child in a quiet mountain valley with time on his hands and the blue sky around him, I don't imagine that mattered very much. The fife was made by burning the pith out of an eight- to ten-inch section of stalk with a hot wire and then plugging one end with wax. Holes were placed along the body to produce different tones.

The fiddle was a bit more complicated but not appreciably more musical. Two identical lengths of stalk were cut about thirteen inches long. Strings were cut right from the body by slitting the stalk lengthwise, stopping just short of the ends. It was slit again, making a "string" about one-eighth inch in diameter (Figure 35). Both stalks were treated the same and one became the body, the other the bow. When the bow was drawn over the strings, it made a sweet kind of wispy drone. I've often wondered if the makers of these fiddles actually intended them to play real music. Of if they were given to a child as we give our toddlers toy steering wheels. For just as driving a car is a very real part of our lives today, fiddle playing was a part of the pioneers'.

SOURCES OF, HARVESTING AND PREPARING CORN

To find corn, drive out into the countryside sometime after Halloween and before Christmas. Try to find a field growing beside a friendly looking farmhouse. Knock on the door and explain your mission—that you would like to have twenty to thirty stalks for craft projects. Depending on the situation, you may be able to obtain such a number without charge. Or you may have to pay. But isn't that the way with everything?

Take along a butcher knife. Corn is equipped with a network of spiderlike roots that appear to have a very tenuous grip on the earth. But those gnarled fingers are as tough as a dog's tooth and can't be pulled out by hand. Cut close to the ground so none of the stalk is wasted.

Before laying out the stalks to dry, strip away the leaves and pull off the ear. The leaves can serve as mulch around plants, and the kernels will make food for winter birds.

Lay the stalks on newspapers to dry and turn occasionally to prevent mildew or mold. Drying will take two or three weeks. They take on a glistening, golden sheen with freckled areas of brown. They are six to eight feet long, one and a half to two inches in diameter at the base, and one-eighth inch at the tips. The stalks are jointed at roughly six- to ten-inch intervals and are filled with a cream-colored fibrous pith.

A coping saw is used to cut the large end of the stalk. Scissors or tin snips serve nicely for the tip end. Holes can be made with a drill or a darning needle.

The husks are cut with scissors and must be soaked to make them pliable. They can be kept moist while you are working with them by placing them in a plastic bag. I found I needed to bleach the husks, maybe not *needed* but wanted to. They will become a creamy white if you soak them for an hour in a scrub bucket to which you've added one cup of regular laundry bleach. Bleaching may take longer, but you can judge for yourself when they've reached the color you want. Rinse well. After they have been bleached they can also be dyed. They take color beautifully. Put into a hot dye bath (Tintex or Rit) and simmer until they reach the right shade. Rinse until the water runs perfectly clear.

The following section is divided into two parts —how to make things from the stalks (canes) and how to make things from the shucks (husks).

CORN STALK ORNAMENTS

GOD EYES (Figure 36)

In Nepal, God Eyes were once hung outside over the door to scare away night-roaming demons. In some parts of Mexico, these eyes were carried to church and placed in a spot where they could look at people while they prayed. I had a feeling when I read this that it was like wanting to keep a portrait of someone you love close by—so you could see each other. Variations of such colorful weavings are nice to make with sections of corn stalks as a base.

MATERIALS AND TOOLS

Paring knife, scissors, glue, a group of slender stalks in varying lengths (according to the size "eye" you want), lengths of colored yarns. If you aren't a "yarn person" you can buy small hanks of woolen yarn normally used for needlepoint and crewel.

PROCEDURE

These directions are for small eyes. You can vary the dimensions to suit your taste.

   1. For each weaving, cut two slender stalks, one

FIGURE 36 *Except for the one large eye, these are all 6 to 8 inches overall. They are so light they can be attached to walls with strips of masking tape. Each of them only takes ten or fifteen minutes to weave from scraps of yarn or twine.*

6" long and the other 8". Lay one over the other so they form a cross. Mark the crossing point with a pencil and scrape away an indentation on the bottom stalk large enough for the top stalk to lie in. Place second stalk in the indentation and begin to wrap yarn around, over and under crossed sticks (Figure 37). Use any number of rows. Reverse the winding occasionally, or go over instead of under to change the design as you go along. Wherever you stop, or need to make a knot, place drop of glue on knot.

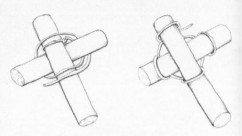

FIGURE 37 *Two different ways of winding yarn around stalks.*

2. When weaving is complete, go back and snip off any loose ends of yarn.

3. Make tassels by winding yarn eight times around three fingers of left hand. Slip off fingers and over end of stalk. Tie in place with small piece of yarn. Place drop of glue on tassel so it won't slide off.

Discarded straight-sided wine bottle, supply of stalks roughly 1" to 2" in diameter, roll of two-sided self-sticking tape (available at hardware stores), 3' or 4' colored raffia or yarn, several cups of sand, skewer.

WEED POT (Figure 38)
MATERIALS

1. Fill wine bottle with sand to make it stable. Wrap tape around bottle in two places—one just above the middle and the other about an inch up from the bottom (Figure 39, left).

PROCEDURE

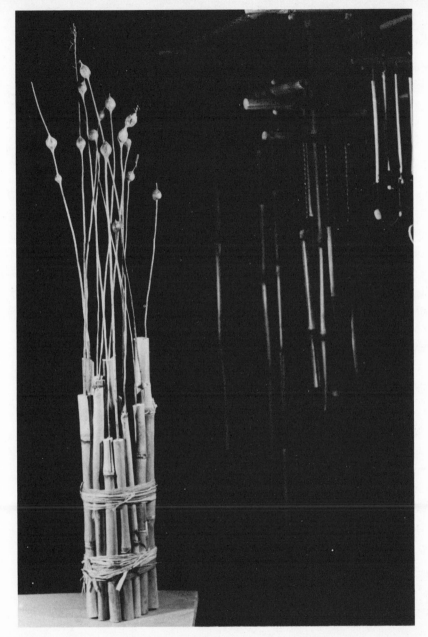

FIGURE 38 *Tall weed pot, left foreground. Corn is like bamboo in appearance and feels silky to the touch. The large hanging in the background was made by lashing four stalks together as a framework and hanging separate removable groups of other stalks to it. Some are decorated with beads of glass and clay.*

2. Measure around bottle to determine how many stalks you will need. Measure height to see how long you need to cut the stalks. Vary the height for visual interest, but make sure the bottle is covered. Cut enough stalks to go around and lay them out on table in the order you want them to appear on the bottle. This bottle required thirteen canes (Figure 39, center).

3. Press canes one by one up against the sticky tape until bottle is covered (Figure 39, right). (A friend's hands would be helpful here.) Whip a length of yarn around the bottle to hold canes in place while you tie it all together with decorative raffia. Wrap raffia as tightly as you can.

4. With a skewer, push one hole down through pith in each cane. Insert one weed in each hole. Place one weed in neck of bottle. If stems are too delicate for pushing, reinforce them with a length of wire wrapped to the stem with florist's tape.

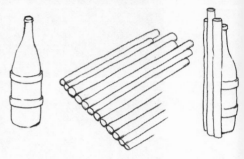

FIGURE 39 *Left to right: Bottle wrapped with two-sided sticky tape. Canes laid out in the order they'll appear on bottle. Bottle partially covered with canes.*

Coping saw, supply of stalks of varying sizes, glue, heavy nylon carpet thread, twelve shucks, darning needle, twelve chestnuts (any nut or pod can be used). The chestnuts have a hole drilled through them for stringing.

CHARM STRING (Figure 40)
MATERIALS AND TOOLS

1. Using a diagonal cut at one end, saw one set of ten stalks 1½″ in diameter and 10″ long; ten stalks of a slightly smaller diameter and approximately

PROCEDURE

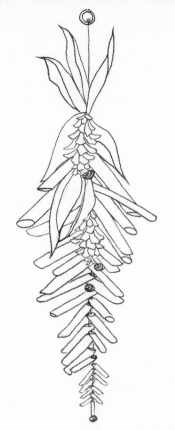

FIGURE 40 *Colors in this charm string range from off-white through gold, brown and patches of silvery green. The whole thing weighs only a few ounces.*

MATERIALS

8″ long; ten stalks of a slightly smaller length and diameter, etc., until you have four groups of stalks, forty in all.

2. Cut one length of carpeting thread 40″ long and tie a loop at one end for hanging. Start threading at this end.

3. Thread needle and, running thread through diagonal end of cane, string largest canes first, medium ones second, etc., until all canes are threaded. At the bottom, run thread through a chestnut and tie in stout knot. Put drop of glue on knot.

4. Thread each chestnut separately on an 8″ thread and tie among the canes as a decorative touch. At top of charm string, tie on six shucks facing up and six shucks facing down. After they are tied, cover the thread with a wrapping of corn shucks made by tearing long strips of shuck ½″ wide. Wrap strips over cord and tuck the stray ends under the wrapping. When dry, glue ends in place. Pine cones were added here for a decorative touch. Straw flowers could be used too.

CORN SHUCK ORNAMENTS

Supply of dampened shucks, cork or foam balls 1″ in diameter, discarded thin bracelets, feathers, felt-tipped markers, glue, needle and nylon thread, piece of heavy cardboard or bulletin board for work surface.

FIGURE 41 *Corn-shuck tree ornaments, left to right, are a bug, a starburst and an angel. In the front is a bird with a real feather tail.*

STARBURST (Figure 41, center left)

PROCEDURE

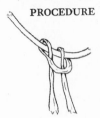

FIGURE 42 *Knotting a length of shuck over wire circle.*

BUG (Figure 41, upper left)

PROCEDURE

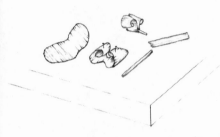

FIGURE 43 *Bug, left to right: Pattern for wings; rolled up and pinned down to dry; folded body. At the top the finished bug flies past an unfolded body.*

BIRD (Figure 41, bottom)

PROCEDURE

1. Tear and cut shucks into strips ½″ wide and 4″ long.

2. Fold in half lengthwise and make a loop in the middle. Lay under ring and bring two ends up through loop and pull tight (Figure 42).

3. Continue adding these loops until ring is covered, pushing each one tightly up against the preceding one.

4. Cover with heavy book or magazines until it dries, then attach thread for hanging.

1. Draw a wing pattern on paper, about 4″ across and 2″ high, using illustration as a guide. Lay this pattern on shuck and draw around and cut out (Figure 43).

2. Roll up outer edges of wings until they meet at the center. Pin to board until they dry.

3. Make a body by folding lengthwise a piece of shuck measuring 2″ long and ¼″ wide. Set it under a weight to dry.

4. Unpin wings, lay body inside wings to make a head and tail. Glue in place. Hold briefly till it dries.

5. Decorate wings with felt-tipped markers and attach thread for hanging.

Roll a strip of damp shuck 1½″ wide and 4″ long into a tight cylinder and pin to board till dry (Figure 44). Tear another strip ½″ wide and 3″ long for the head. Fold in half lengthwise and roll up tightly. Pin down to dry. When both parts are dry, glue a little sliver to top of back to make a "wing." Stitch head to body with two stitches. Place a drop of glue on feathers and push inside body. Hold there a minute to dry and attach thread for hanging.

1. Cover foam ball with three damp husks about 5″ long and 3″ wide. Tie at bottom of ball to form neck (Figure 45).

2. Take two more strips 8″ long and 3″ wide and lay one on each side of head to form wings. Tie at neck.

3. Fan out shucks and trim into wing shapes while still wet. Lay on table and pin down wings until dry. Attach thread for hanging.

In addition to a large supply of shucks (about two grocery-sackfuls), you will need a plastic basket made for hanging plants. They are sold in florists' shops and cost about a dollar. The rims are drilled for hanging. You will also need a spool of 28-gauge wire to cut into 8″ lengths and several handfuls of moss to line the finished basket. Moss can be purchased from plant shops or collected on walks in the forest.

Tear and cut dampened shucks into strips ½″ wide and 4″ long (Figure 46). Put both ends of three strips together and secure at bottom with an 8″

FIGURE 44 *Left to right, front: Rolled-up body; rolled-up head; wings cut from flat piece of shuck. Top, finished bird.*

ANGEL (Figure 41, right)
PROCEDURE

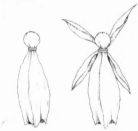

FIGURE 45 *Corn-husk angel, left, with cord tied at neck to make head. Right, finished angel with her wings tied on.*

HANGING BASKET WITH BRAIDED ROPE
MATERIALS

PROCEDURE

FIGURE 46 *Top left, flower-like bundle; bottom left, bundle secured to basket with wire, inside view. Right, basket as it begins to sprout the bundles.*

length of wire. This forms a little flowerlike bundle. Push ends of bundle through holes in basket (with the flower on the outside), and secure to basket by wrapping wires around openings in basket. Go over whole basket till it is completely covered, then go back and secure wires by pushing them into each other and clipping off unnecessary lengths. Line interior of finished basket with moss. It can then be used for a hanging plant. A wire can be used to hang the basket, but it is easy to braid a sturdy rope from husks. Tear husks into ½″ widths as long as the husk is long. Place three strips side by side, tie one set of ends together and then place over a nail on a work surface. Braid strips as you would braid hair. Add new strips when they're needed, overlapping the strips at least 1½″ so they won't pull out. Move rope up on nail as it gets too long. Go back over rope when done and clip away loose ends. Keep husks damp while working.

Making Paper from Plants and Flowers

I can tell you how to do it, but I don't really understand the technique of making paper. No, that's wrong. I understand the technique but don't know why it works. Each time I go through the steps and discover a nice wet sheet of paper lying on the table before me, I'm totally amazed. If anyone's around to listen, I'm apt to say triumphantly, "Isn't that *something!*" Even if no one's there, I've been known to say the same thing. It's lovely to feel such triumph, but I don't know why I should be so astonished. Simple, everyday people have been making paper for centuries. Beautiful, useful paper from thistles, leaves, bark, grasses—even cabbage. The ancient Egyptians laid thinly sliced strips of the papyrus plant side by side and produced sheets of paper that were subsequently polished with stone. Bamboo was also used in this fashion. And though they were not paper in the strictest sense, clay, stone, hides, bark and copper have all been written on.

During the present technological age, paper has changed dramatically from the first fragile sheets credited to a craftsman in first-century China. The addition of various chemicals has given us paper that will not burn; that will either completely disappear when wet or survive a drenching; that can be stretched, woven, eaten, washed, dry-cleaned and sewn into disposable clothing to wear to the moon. As you can see, the making of paper has become a complex and highly technical process—a far, far distance from papyrus and cabbage leaves. This may be the reason why present-day craftsmen have been reluctant to tackle it. Other handcrafts like weaving and pottery have survived one century after another, but artists making handmade paper are now almost nonexistent in the United States.

In Japan, however, the art never really disappeared. The output today isn't voluminous, but craftsmen in small villages continue to make paper using most of the old-time, lengthy techniques. It may be just personal bias, but I believe Japanese papers are more beautiful than those made by anyone else. Booklets containing samples of their paper are so beautiful they can be purchased as works of art. At Aiko's, an art materials shop in Chicago, you can buy large, inexpensive sheets that can be displayed on the wall, unframed and unexplained. Some of them are so soft it is possible to tie-dye them. There are lacy sheets of delicate pastels, sheets with chunks of bark and twigs imbedded in them, and some that have brightly polished or oiled surfaces.

MAKING PAPER AT HOME

I have tried very few art processes that yield a pleasing product the first time around. But making paper is an exception. The initial sheet wasn't one that I would write to my senator on, but it was a dazzling, raggedy fragment that made me feel happy all day long. I wanted to write "I love you" on it and send it around the world (Figure 47).

Before you begin to make paper, it would be good to understand a little about its nature. Tear a corner from a sheet of typing paper or stationery and you will observe, through a magnifying glass, that tiny fibers protrude all along the torn edge. These fibers come either from rags or from wood pulp. The finest, most expensive papers are made

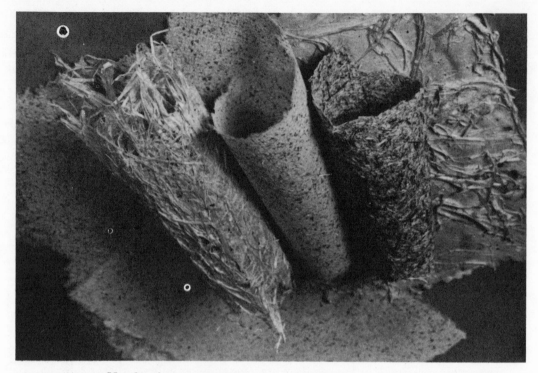

FIGURE 47   *Handmade paper made from riverbank grass, nasturtiums and gourd vines. The first two are pale shades of green, while the fibrous-appearing gourd paper is pink. Handmade papers can be smooth enough to write on, or rich in texture.*

from rags, while newspapers, magazines and most stationery are made from wood pulp. Because most growing plants have a fibrous cellular structure, it is a relatively simple process for us to take plants and turn them into pulp for paper.

A simplified, step-by-step explanation of the process goes like this: Raw plant material is gathered and cut into short lengths. It is then macerated and mixed with water in a vat. A mold is dipped into this solution and when it comes out of the water it has captured a layer of pulp on the surface. When the pulp dries, it is peeled off as a sheet of paper. This section will demonstrate: (1) how to make paper using scratch paper combined with plants, (2) how to make paper using plants alone, and (3) how to color and decorate it.

The tools can be found in most kitchens and consist of a large pan for boiling plants, a blender or mixer, a large sieve, an iron, and a vessel large and deep enough to dip the mold in and out of. A five-gallon galvanized bucket serves very well. A plastic dishpan or baby bathtub will work too. In addition to these kitchen things, you will need to make a mold or set of molds. You can make one by stretching a piece of thin fabric such as organdy over a small wooden frame (Figure 48). Embroidery hoops also make interesting molds. They come in a variety of sizes and shapes and only need a piece of fabric stretched over them.

Raw Material. Because he hoped to find a substitute for the expensive cotton and linen fibers being used, Dr. Jacob Christian Schaeffer began experimenting with ordinary plants in the early 1700s. He documented experiments with almost eighty different materials. Among them were corn

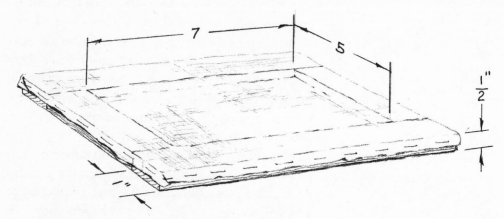

FIGURE 48   *A very thin fabric like organdy, voile or nylon is stapled to a simple wooden frame. It should be taut so the sheets will be smooth.*

husks, thistles, cattail stalks, pine cones, tree leaves, reeds, cabbage leaves and potatoes. This information came from a book written by John Mason, a British craftsman. *Paper Making as an Artistic Craft* describes Mason's experiments with plants gathered from the English countryside. He used rushes, grasses, gladioluses, irises and nettles. As for me, I have used peony leaves and stems, long grasses from riverbanks, birch bark, nasturtiums, gourd vines and wild iris leaves. There are very few growing things, it seems, that can't be turned into pulp.

MAKING PULP
PROCEDURE

From my own experience I have found that suc-culent plants or the fleshy parts of plants yield the least desirable fibers. Conversely, stems and leaves produce the best. It is wise to use plants when they are green rather than dried.

1. When the material is gathered, lay it out on a chopping board or on sheets of paper on the floor. Cut it into 1″ to 2″ lengths with a butcher knife or scissors.

2. Place the chopped material in a pot of water (water to cover) and boil with lye (1 tablespoon per quart of water). Lye helps dissolve the fleshy, nonfibrous matter.

3. Boil until the plants become soft and mushy-looking. The time varies with the plant, but nor-mally this means about ten minutes.

4. Pour off lye water through a sieve and rinse carefully so you don't wash away tiny fibers. Lye burns, so use rubber gloves or be very careful.

5. Place small amount of rinsed pulp into blender with just enough water to blend. Mix at fast speed for a few seconds and repeat until you have blended (macerated) all the material. Tough fibers require more macerating than fragile ones, of course.

This then, is your basic pulp—the material that you will add to a vat of water.

1. Have 6 to 8 quarts of water ready in a large container and add prepared pulp to this, all at one time. Stir.

2. Take mold and, holding it in both hands so it is level, dip it into the vat with a sweeping motion that brings your hands up on the side away from you (Figure 49). Then, all in the same motion, bring mold straight up out of the water, allowing it to capture and hold a thin layer of the pulp on the screen. If the layer is too thin, dip it back into vat, stir and repeat dipping procedure. If it's too thick, rinse pulp back into vat and repeat. It takes just a few times to give you an idea of the technique. Stir the pulp each time before you dip. You will note that the mixture gets thinner and thinner as you dip away the fibers. You might want to have more pulp on hand and add it, a cup at a time.

3. Allow excess water to drain back into the vat and then set aside mold to allow paper to dry. (See other drying directions that follow on page 103–104.)

4. Lift paper at corner and peel off.

Schoolchildren in Boston recently celebrated ecology day by making paper from old notepaper plus such vegetable parts as lettuce, cabbage and carrot leaves, and the peelings from potatoes and cucumbers. This is a very simple process and the following is a variation of it.

FORMING SHEETS
PROCEDURE

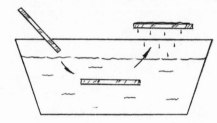

FIGURE 49 *A smooth scooping motion will deposit an even covering of pulp on the mold.*

RECIPE FOR NASTURTIUM PAPER

PROCEDURE

1. Gather 2 quarts of nasturtium leaves and stems. Throw in an occasional nasturtium too, not because you need to but because they look so spicy among the green leaves. Cut into 1" lengths.

2. Pour 2 cups of water into electric blender and gradually add four sheets of white typing paper that have been shredded. Blend until soft and mushy and all traces of shreds have disappeared.

3. Add a handful of freshly chopped nasturtium stuff at a time, and blend. Keep adding and blending until you have about 3 cups of pulp in the blender. These proportions are quite flexible. You can vary them considerably without harm.

4. Add pulp to vat and form sheets according to directions, page 100.

This recipe makes about a dozen sheets of 5" x 7" notepaper. It is a delicate green with shreds of darker green throughout. If you hold it up to the light, you can see light and dark areas indicating spots where fibers have become thicker in some parts than others. This is good.

RECIPE FOR IRIS PAPER

Unlike the nasturtium paper, which has a base of recycled paper pulp, iris paper is made entirely from plant fibers. The sheets are a pale rosy-brown, somewhat like the color of brown eggs. There are threads of very dark green scattered throughout.

PROCEDURE

Gather two large grocery-sackfuls of raw material—in this case, iris leaves. Cut only a few leaves from each growing plant so you don't leave ugly scars. Cut leaves into 1″ and 2″ lengths and place in a pot of water with lye. Proceed according to directions for making pulp, page 99. Place pulp in vat of water and begin to form sheets according to directions on page 100.

NOTE: You may want to make paper from iris leaves by skipping the boiling-with-lye steps. This will give you an entirely different kind of paper. It will be a shaggy, tweedy outdoor green. It can't be used for writing, but the sheets look magnificent when light comes through them. I glued squares of them on my office window in a checkerboard pattern, alternating them with sheets made of peony leaves. The peony paper is a rose-brown and looks like it should smell of cinnamon. It has a rough, curly surface.

Drying Paper. Strangely enough, drying the sheets of paper was the trickiest part of the whole process. The simplest method of drying is to let the pulp dry right on the mold. It takes a long time, though, and you can only make a few sheets at a time this way. Because I made a set of four molds, I was able to nip the sheets into the oven like cookies. They dry in about five minutes. Set the temperature at 250 degrees Fahrenheit and leave the door just slightly ajar. Lay the mold right on the open shelves and put a sheet of foil on the oven floor to catch any drippings. When the paper is dry it changes color and gives a slight crackly

sound when you tap it with your nail. Slip a fingernail under one corner and peel it off slowly. Then
lay the sheet on the ironing board, set temperature
control to lowest setting, and press as you would
any delicate fabric. The pressing gives the sheets
a barely perceptible gloss.

John Mason, whose book I mentioned earlier,
uses a more traditional way of drying paper. It's
very efficient and, in the end, I think it's less trouble
than oven-drying.

In the paper-making trade, this system of drying
is called "couching" (a little like putting children
down for a nap). The newly formed sheets of
paper are laid on squares of wet felt two or three
inches larger all around than the dimensions of the
paper. Each new sheet of paper is piled on top of
the previous one with a sheet of wet felt in between. When the pile is completed, the excess water is squeezed out by a press.

In order to try this system, cut a stack of felts
from felt from a fabric store. Or try any heavy
fabric with a discernible nap. I discovered that an
old woolen blanket made a good substitute for
felt.

1. Wet the felts and stack them beside your
work table (Figure 50). When first sheet is ready,
lay the edge of mold directly on a single felt and,
using a sideways rocking motion, press paper into
felt. Lift mold, leaving sheet of paper behind.

2. Set felt aside till you do the next sheet, and

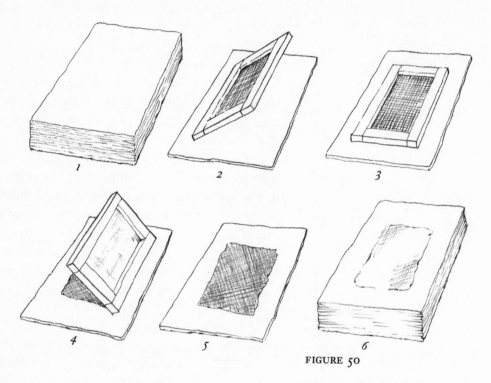

FIGURE 50

1. Wet felts stacked beside table
2. Mold is rocked onto the felt
3. Then pressed down
4. Mold is lifted
5. Sheet of paper is left behind
6. Felts are stacked one on top of the other.

then stack one on top of the other. Continue until you have the number of sheets you want, and then place a board on top of pile; lay it on the floor and step on it to press out water.

3. Unstack felts and remove sheets to continue drying on a flat surface.

4. Iron.

DECORATING THE SHEETS

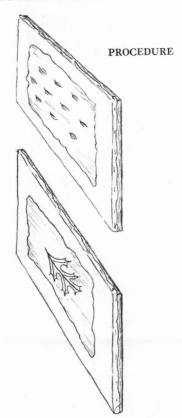

PROCEDURE

FIGURE 51 *Small delicate twigs, leaves, etc., will become part of the paper when they are covered with a small amount of pulp.*

Most plants, not surprisingly, give varying shades of brown and green. If you want to change the color, the fibers must first be bleached.

1. To bleach fibers, put them through the cutting and boiling-with-lye process. Rinse and put in a glass jar with liquid laundry bleach. Fill a quart jar loosely with pulp and add water to within two inches of the top. Add liquid bleach to fill the jar and let it stand overnight or until the fibers have bleached to your satisfaction.

2. Rinse away bleach water through a sieve.

3. Proceed, using directions for making pulp, and then place pulp in vat. Using small bottles of food coloring, add a few drops of color to the pulp in the vat. The fibers absorb the color immediately, so you can check it as you go, adding more color a drop or two at a time until you have the color you want. Stir thoroughly and often as you work.

Sheets can be decorated while they're still lying wet on the mold. Lay a wet skeletonized leaf, delicate twig, feather or colored thread right on the wet pulp (Figure 51). Holding mold over the vat, reach in with one hand and bring up a handful of new pulp and drip it slowly over the leaf. This acts like a lid, or the top layer of a sandwich. Dry and press as usual.

(NOTE: To skeletonize leaves, pick while green and boil five to ten minutes in a lye bath, one tablespoon of lye per quart of water. Rinse in cool water. Lay leaf on rim of sink and brush away the pulpy material with an old, soft toothbrush. The veins and capillaries of the leaf will remain in a delicate framework of lines.)

When sheets are couched according to Mason's system, it is easy to decorate them with added materials. One sheet is couched onto the felt and the wetted decorative object placed directly on it. Then a second, very thin sheet is couched right over the first one. Make the second sheet as thin as possible so the decorative material will show through.

Using Plants to Make Dyes

One of the surest but saddest ways to add color to a piece of fabric is to spill coffee or tea on it. But it's a lot more satisfying to ease it into a pot of dye made from the good juices of berries, bark or leaves. Extracting rich colors from plant material is neither mysterious nor difficult—although it does seem almost a miracle to transfer the color from a hickory nut or a geranium to a skein of yarn.

Until about a hundred and twenty years ago, when synthetic dyes were discovered, the only ones available were those made of natural materials: dyes that came from seashells, insects, roots, lichen, galls, nuts and fruit. Dyeing was a lengthy and time-consuming process that could never become an exact science because of the nature of nature. Each plant the craftsman worked with was influenced by the soil in which it grew, by whether or not the sun shone on it all day or only a part of it, and by how much rain fell during the year. So dye made from two of the same kind of plants but grown in two different localities would produce two different hues of the same color, or maybe even two different colors. In addition, fleece varied from sheep to sheep, so the wool reacted to the dye in a variety of ways.

Since "fixers" were also required to set the dyes, they added yet another element of uncertainty. Temperatures of dye baths and the chemical content of the water were also factors that limited standardization. Even so, some of the recipes for dyes that have survived in historical journals show that dyers made a supreme effort to maintain control over all these variables. And the beautiful textiles we see in museums today indicate that their colors have remained steadfast and true, century after century.

Throughout history, color seems to have been almost as essential to people's existence as food. Dye workshops were conducted in China three thousand years before the birth of Christ. The ancient Egyptians, Phoenicians and East Indians were all concerned with color. And later on, new Americans showed interest too. At a time when they were almost totally engaged in the struggle to simply stay alive, they found time to put color into their daily lives. Packets of seed for growing dye-stuff arrived on ships along with the colonists. Other packets were ordered later from the Old World. After there was time, and life spread out in a more leisurely pattern, women started growing their own color gardens or went out and brought home the materials that grew in the countryside. Among other things, they used butternuts, sassafras bark and elderberries. To give their hand-woven pieces variety, housewives sometimes set up looms using one color of yarn for the warp and another for the woof. They even used a variation of tie-dyeing, a process that is so popular today. They tied lengths of string around hanks of yarn. After pulling them tight, so the dye couldn't reach these sections, the yarn was tossed into a dye pot and left to steep for several weeks. The result was a varicolored scarf or pair of socks.

In spite of the time required and the uncertainties of the results, many people today have become fascinated with the old-fashioned process of making dyes from natural materials (Figure 52). Experts at the Smithsonian Institution seem bemused by the fact that some people apparently derive pleasure from the old processes for the very

FIGURE 52 *The yarn in the basket has all been handspun and dyed by weaver Delle Gherity. Among other plants, she used wild parsnip, black walnut, and Queen Anne's lace.*

reason they were rejected. Many universities offer classes in the old methods as part of their weaving curriculum. A number of artists and private schools give workshops that last from one day to a whole summer. Some of them begin out in the open field with the plants and go through all the steps of sheep-shearing, carding, spinning and then dyeing. A great part of the attraction of natural dyes, according to the devotees, is that they never change color. They may fade, but they won't "gray" as synthetic dyes are apt to do. They also "marry well," a term used to convey the fact that no color disagrees with the color next to it. In a basket containing a dozen different hues and colors, all seem to be in perfect harmony with one another.

The process of dyeing with natural dyes can be summed up as follows: Raw material is gathered, crushed, boiled and then strained. The textile or fiber is mordanted, immersed in the dye, simmered, rinsed and then dried. Cotton, wool, linen, feathers, leather, straw—anything that needs to be colored can be dyed with natural dyes.

EXAMPLES OF PLANTS AND NOTES ON GATHERING

When gathering plant material, plan to collect flowers, leaf tips or berries when they seem to be at their peak. Roots and bark give their best colors when gathered in the fall. All of them can be dried and stored for later use. Tie in fairly loose bunches and either hang head-down or spread out on newspapers in a dry spot. Label everything so you can duplicate your efforts if you fall in love with one color.

I have counted over a hundred natural materials that can be used to make color. I would guess, though, that there aren't *any* plants which haven't been tried at one time or another. To give you an idea of the colors that can be extracted, check the following list:

Goldenrod	yellow
Willow bark	rose-tan
Sassafras flower	yellow
Sassafras root or bark	rose-brown
Horseradish leaves	yellow, yellow-brown
Onion skins	brown, burnt orange
Sunflower seeds	blue
Madder	red
Indigo	blue
Birch bark	red
Wild plum bark	red
Pomegranate rinds	yellow

EXTRACTING AND DYEING

Large enamel pot—20- to 30-gallon size—wooden or glass stirring rod, kitchen scales, sieve, cheesecloth, supply of soft water (4 gallons to each pound of yarn or cloth), plant material.

EQUIPMENT AND MATERIALS

NOTE: Household water softeners provide what is meant here by soft water. Rain water is also excellent for this purpose, as is distilled water.

PROCEDURE

Each recipe varies as to times and proportions, but the basic procedure is as follows: Blossoms, berries or green plants are crushed and then boiled in soft water, just to cover. Bark, roots, nuts or other heavy fibrous materials are soaked overnight and then boiled. This creates the liquid dye, which is then strained through a sieve and then again through cheesecloth. The dye liquid is ready to use immediately. It can also be poured into glass or plastic containers and stored in the refrigerator. If it is to be stored for more than twenty-four hours, add 1 teaspoon sodium of benzoate to 1 gallon of hot dye. It can then be stored for at least two weeks—possibly more, but I haven't done any experiments past the two-week period myself. Dye can also be frozen, but it may lose some intensity of color. If frozen, it can be kept almost indefinitely.

The material to be dyed is weighed while it is dry and 4 gallons of dye bath allowed for each pound of material. Yarn is tied into loose bundles. Fabric is shaken out loosely. It is then wetted thoroughly, placed in the dye bath, and slowly brought to a boil. While it is simmering, it is frequently turned and lifted to make sure the dye penetrates all the fibers. If the water level drops too low, the material can be lifted out, more water added to cover, and then returned to the pot. It is simmered till the desired color is reached. It can be left to cool in the dye bath or removed and rinsed immediately. It is rinsed thoroughly until the water runs clear.

MORDANTING

The term "mordant" comes from the Latin "mordere," which means to bite. In other words, its function is to grab the color and hang on for dear life. A number of different mordants are used in the dyeing process, the most widely used being alum (aluminum potassium sulphate). Some others are chrome (potassium dichromate), tannic acid or copperas (ferrous sulfate). They can also be extracted from oak galls and sumac leaves.

Mordants are needed to *set* color, but they can also be used to *change* color. This fact is illustrated in the book *Natural Dyes in the United States*, as the author explains that a chrome mordant used with dahlia flowers will color wool orange. If alum is used, the wool will be a light yellow.

Since alum is the most widely used mordant, a recipe is given here for its use with wool. You will need 4 ounces of alum, 1 ounce of cream of tartar, and 4 gallons of soft water for each pound of fabric or yarn.

For one pound of wool, place 4 ounces of alum

PROCEDURE

and 1 ounce of cream of tartar in a large kettle of water. Wet the wool, squeeze out excess water and add to the kettle. Heat slowly to boiling point and boil gently for one hour, lifting and turning wool so the mordant penetrates all the fibers. If water level drops, add more water so the wool will continue to be covered. Remove from heat and let stand in kettle overnight. After rinsing, it is ready for the dye bath. Mordanted material can be set aside and dyed at a later time, but it shouldn't wait more than seventy-two hours.

Cotton is mordanted in the same fashion as wool except that 1 ounce of washing soda (available in grocery stores) is substituted for the cream of tartar.

DYE RECIPES

The following recipes have all been tested. They will give you a starting point from which to begin your own experiments in dyeing. Wash any material to be dyed in sudsy water and rinse thoroughly. When handling wool, it's important to know that abrupt changes in temperature will harm the wool fibers. Always reduce or increase temperatures gradually.*

* The following two recipes are printed here with the permission of Rita J. Adrosko, Curator, Division of Textiles, Smithsonian Institution. They can be found in her book *Natural Dyes in the United States* (Washington, D.C.: Smithsonian Institution, 1968).

Pecan Hulls (Carya illinoensis or Hicoria pecan)
Pecan trees grow in Iowa, Indiana and the
Southern States

Brown Wool: alum mordant

1 pound wool
¾ peck green pecan hulls
   Use alum mordant. Cut the hulls from nuts and boil them in water for 15 minutes. Strain and add cold water to make a dyebath of 4 to 4½ gallons. Before immersing mordanted wool in the dyebath, thoroughly rinse it and squeeze out excess moisture. Immerse the wool; gradually heat the dyebath to boiling; boil for 30 minutes, rinse and dry.

Dark Gray Cotton: alum mordant

1 pound cotton
¾ peck green pecan hulls
⅙ oz. ferrous sulfate (copperas)
   Use alum mordant. Follow directions for dyeing "Brown Wool" (above). Without rinsing, transfer the cotton into a boiling bath of ferrous sulfate in 4 gallons of water. Stir, continuing to boil for 10 minutes, rinse and dry.

Viburnum Leaves (Viburnum tomentosium mariesi). A large grocery bag packed loosely with leaves was gathered on July 12, 1972. It was a very wet summer, temperatures below average, shrub shaded for part of the day, and the soil above average in fertility. The leaves were torn

ROSE WOOL: *Alum Mordant*

up a bit and placed in a 20-quart enamel canning kettle and soft water added to just cover the leaves. The pot was brought to the simmer point and allowed to simmer for one and a quarter hours. (The dye bath has an odor similar to that of cooking raspberries and quite pleasant. The viburnums are a member of the honeysuckle family.) The bath will turn red *gradually* and, as it cools, will turn a clearer, brighter red much like the color of Chianti wine. It is important that the color be extracted slowly and the pot never go beyond the low simmer point. In my experience, red dyes deteriorate quickly at high and prolonged extraction. After the bath was cooled, it was strained, placed in a plastic gallon container, and frozen for future use.

A month later, a skein of alum-mordanted Hampshire yarn was entered into a lukewarm dye bath and simmered for thirty minutes. The skein was removed and 2⅔ tablespoons Glauber's salts (dissolved in 1 pint of hot water) was added to the 1-gallon dye bath. The skein was reentered and allowed to simmer for an additional thirty minutes. It cooled in the dye bath and was rinsed six times—until the color stopped bleeding.

CLEAR, LIME-GREEN WOOL:
Alum Mordant

Korean Littleleaf Boxwood (*Buxus microphylla,* var. *Koreana*). Four loosely packed quarts of tip clippings were taken from the shrub on September 21, 1972. This was a very wet summer, temperatures below normal, and the shrub growing in full sun in relatively fertile soil. However, being close to a house foundation, it had not been in an acid soil, and this was evident from the fact that the shrub tended to have a yellow-green coloration.

The clippings were placed in an 8-quart enamel pot after being bruised somewhat, covered with soft water, and allowed to soak overnight. The next day the clippings were allowed to simmer in the same water for about one and a half hours. The dye bath was strained, allowed to cool to lukewarm, and a skein of wetted-out, alum-mordanted Hampshire yarn was entered. It was allowed to simmer in the dye bath for one hour, cooled in the bath and rinsed three times.

The above two recipes are the result of experiments by Delle Gherity. Delle spins her own wool and weaves textiles and tapestries. She is a meticulous craftswoman.

Red *

Boil for an hour ½ the weight of the wool being dyed, the roots of Ladies Bedstraw in water to cover. Boiled first in the alum solution it gives an orange-red, with the bichromate solution a crimson. Beet Red: mordant wool with alum and boil in beet juice.

* This recipe is from *The Book of Country Crafts* (Cranbury, New Jersey: A. S. Barnes and Co., Inc., 1964) by Randolph Wardell Johnston, and is used with the permission of the publisher.

NOTE: Ladies Bedstraw is a weed that grows prolifically along fence rows and roadsides. It can also be ordered from one of the sources listed on page 195.

DEEP GOLD DENIM:
Alum Mordant

FIGURE *53 Top, several beans are tied securely with twine into a tight ball. Bottom, sunbursts of white appear in the deep gold fabric where the twine was wrapped.*

Marigold Flowers. Wash 1 yard new white denim in hot sudsy water, rinse thoroughly and then mordant according to directions for mordanting cotton, page 113. Dry.

Rather than dye the denim a solid color, I decided to try to create the same effect as the traditional "plangi" fabrics that are made by artists in certain parts of Africa. They tie off areas of cloth to keep the dye from penetrating at these points. As a result, the tied-off areas create sunbursts of undyed fabric.

To make this kind of pattern myself, I spread out the denim after it was mordanted and placed pencil dots where I wanted the sunbursts to appear. At each of these points, I placed several large dry Italian beans (Figure 53). (Any nice dry bean will do.) The fabric was drawn around the beans and sewn tightly into a ball with nylon carpeting thread. Then several lengths of thread were wrapped around the base of the bean ball and tied off with a stout knot.

The tied-up fabric, complete with its beans, was wetted and placed in dye bath made from 3 pecks of fresh marigolds. To make the marigold dye, gather the flowers and wash them, outside if you can. They will probably have ladybugs in them and you wouldn't want to take them inside. They're not unfriendly but if you leave them outside they can fly away and eat bad bugs that destroy vegetables. Drop the flowers into a pot of soft water to cover and bring to boil. Boil for twenty minutes. The kitchen will smell like . . . well, like marigolds. Strain brew through strainer and then through cloth and add soft water to make a dye bath in the proportion of 4 gallons of bath to 1 pound of fabric. Place wet fabric in dye bath, bring to boil, and boil for fifteen minutes. Lift and turn fabric often. Rinse in one water after another until the water is completely clear. When dry, clip away threads and remove beans. Press. The fabric will be a deep, deep gold with sunbursts of variegated white to gold.

SOURCES FOR CHEMICALS, SUPPLIES, ETC.

The chemicals needed for dyeing and mordanting may be available from your neighborhood drugstore. This is the easiest place to start, but if they aren't carried there and can't be ordered for you, here are mail-order sources:

1. Natural Dye Supplies, P.O. Box 7, Pelham, New York 10803.

2. Lamb's End, 16861 Hamilton, Highland Park, Michigan 48203.

If you want to try some dyes from plant materials but don't have the plants, check the yellow pages of your telephone directory for listings under Botanicals or Herbs. Buying bark, herbs, etc., can be expensive, but it will give you a chance to try out small amounts of some particular dye. But do remember that even ordinary hedges and shrubbery are excellent sources of color. The Indiana Botanic Gardens, 626 177th Street, Hammond, Indiana 46325, has a price list they'll send that gives a number of botanicals such as barberry bark, bugleweed, burdock, stinging nettle, dwarf elder and bark.

The Faribault Woolen Mills, Faribault, Minnesota 55021, is a source for scoured wool. This means fleece that has been cleaned and is ready for hand-spinning. They will sell by mail if you can tell them what kind of wool you want and how much. Lamb's End (above) also sells natural yarns (undyed) and other fibers for spinning and dyeing.

ADDITIONAL NOTES

Because natural dyes are most often spoken of in relation to weaving and spinning, many people may feel their use is limited. But they can be used for anything that you want colored—feathers, straw, grasses, corn husks, yard goods and commercial yarns. Anyone who enjoys knitting or crocheting may buy plain white yarn and dye it just as hand-spuns are dyed. For yard goods, it's best to stick with wool or cotton. The synthetics are a whole other ball game.

Gourds are absurd. They're not a fruit—exactly. They're not a vegetable, though some may be eaten as such. And they're definitely not a berry. About the only thing you can say with certainty is that gourds grow on vines, have a woody outer shell, and come in a lot of funny shapes. Some are tiny golden spheres. Many have warts and moles all over their bodies with varicose veins that look like they might be painful. Others have necks reaching from here clear down to the ground. They're a delightfully democratic plant, for their sex practices are uninhibited and they're happy to mate with almost any other gourd, squash or pumpkin. So what you plant may not be what you get. But that's okay. I think gourds have more fun than any other plant, and more honest beauty.

Their loony-shaped, adaptable bodies have been put to use throughout history in so many ways that it almost seems that civilization couldn't have proceeded at an orderly pace without them. Where did they come from? No one knows for sure. But a good indication of their lineage is the fact that they were uncovered in Egyptian tombs dated 3300 B.C. Even when gourds were used for mundane purposes, people treated them as art objects.

Gourds Become Ornaments and Entertainments for the Eye and Hand

It seems no one could resist drawing pictures on them or decorating them in some fashion. The Hopi Indians in the southwestern United States stored grain in huge, highly decorated gourds that were about the size of a half-bushel basket. The Japanese decorated a bottle-shaped species that they used as a wine decanter. The Chinese put small ones to use as cages for their pet crickets. I don't know if they still follow this practice, but traditionally it was thought that crickets brought good luck. They were kept outside during the summer (in pottery jars), but in the fall they were taken in and placed in houses made from tiny gourds. These "houses," which can be seen at the Peabody Museum in Salem, Massachusetts, were decorated while they were still growing. A mold with a pattern carved in it was placed around the gourd. As it grew larger, the gourd filled the mold and the pattern was incised on its skin. Tops for the containers were carved from wood or ivory. Using only the natural materials at hand, unknown craftsmen all over Africa turned gourds into works of art. Bowls, ladles, water bottles, pitchers, and so on were stained deep reds, blues and rosy hues. Or they kept the natural color of the gourd and incised a pattern into its skin like a tattoo. Sometimes areas of the skin were scraped away and colors rubbed on the surface. Craftsmen in Peru incised a design and then rubbed colors into the incision (Figure 54).

Make-it-or-do-without settlers in early America

FIGURE 54 *Bowl with a lid and decorative fish—two Peruvian gourds from the collection of First People, Chicago, a gallery that presents the work of native craftsmen.*

put the gourd to dozens of practical uses but, as far as I know, never laid a hand on one to decorate it. What the Americans lacked in a desire for artistic confrontation they made up for in the variety of uses they expected of this creature. A visitor to a mountain cabin in the early 1900s found them being used to hold soda, salt, sugar, flour, soft soap and grease. In those days they were also made into horns to call people (or sheep) in to dinner. They were carried as powder horns when a cow horn wasn't available and, of course, for dippers to hang beside the well. One of their most delightful and inventive uses was for fiddles and banjos. Gourd banjos were fairly commonplace in the southern hills, and many well-known folk musicians today "larned off" on an instrument made from a gourd, a coon hide, and a few hairs from a horse's tail.

MAKING GIFTS FROM GOURDS

Gourds are amiable. They *want* to be used. They can be painted, dyed, carved, drilled, scorched, sawed, glued and sewn. I'm going to assume now that you have gourds you've bought from a farmer's market, the supermarket or a mail-order house. They usually are harvested in late September. (At the end of the chapter there are some hints for growing them yourself.) The gourds you find in the fall will need to dry for three to six months, maybe longer. After you use them for decorative purposes, you can move them to a dry place to begin the drying process. Lay them on papers or hang them in one of the mesh bags onions and potatoes are sold in. As they begin to dry, they do all kinds of terrible-looking things. They ooze and weep and grow hideous patches of mold. But it's a healthy, honorable process that needs understanding. Some people have thought their gourds were suffering a terminal illness and threw them away at this point. Trust them. They'll feel just fine once they're through drying. The smaller they are, the quicker they dry, of course, and there should be some to work with by December.

Preparing Gourds. Soak the gourds you want to work with for fifteen or twenty minutes and then scrub as you would a dirty dish—using mild detergent and a pot scrubber. When they're dry, cut them open and remove the seeds. Save for planting in the spring. The interior has a soft ivory color and a velvety sheen. If you want to remove this velvet layer, soak the gourd again and scrape away the tissue with a spoon. You will feel the difference in texture when you reach the outer woody skin.

Cutting Gourds. Pocket or craft knife, hacksaw with a thin blade, electric or hand drill, file.   TOOLS

Draw cutting line on dry gourd with a pencil. Go over the line several times with tip of pocket knife. When the line is established, either continue with   PROCEDURE pocket knife until cut through completely, or switch to thin-bladed hacksaw. Work slowly, gradually applying pressure. If the gourd breaks, it *can* be glued, but it won't break if you work carefully. When cutting large areas, holes can be drilled at intervals along pencil line. Work between holes with knife.

Decorating Gourds. Basic decorating materials used here are: white glue, sandpaper, acrylic paints, felt-tipped marking pens with permanent colors, Metallic Luster Wax, can of foam walnut wood stain, brushing and spray lacquers, beads, feathers, nuts.

The tools, materials and procedures for the gifts in Figure 55 and those that follow are much the same. The directions are meant only as a guide. Feel free to make any alterations or additions you want.

HANGING MASK (Figure 55)

The mask was made from the discarded top of the ceremonial bowl in the same illustration. It is 6 inches in diameter.

PROCEDURE

1. Smooth the cut edges with a file and sandpaper.

2. Rub several coats of walnut stain into the skin with a soft cloth until you reach the color you want. Dry between coats.

3. Draw face with pencil, then paint with acrylics, felt-tipped pens or both.

4. When dry, spray with six very fine coats of

FIGURE 55 *Objects made from gourds. At bottom, three small wine cups; left, a ceremonial bowl; right, a beach bag; hanging at the rear is a decorative mask. They are all decorated with easy-to-use acrylic paints and felt-tipped marking pens.*

lacquer. Spray cautiously at first so the colors won't run.

5. Glue hair in place with white glue. This hair was from an old Halloween wig. Yarn or twine could be used effectively too.

6. Thumbtack a loop of string to back of mask for hanging.

WINE CUPS (Figure 55) Wine cups are 3 inches in diameter and have flat bottoms that won't tip.

PROCEDURE

1. Cut tops from gourds, remove seeds, scrape inside of gourds until smooth, and smooth edges with sandpaper.

2. Apply eight separate coats of brushing lacquer to interior of the cups. Pour in a small amount at a time, swish it around to cover, and then pour out immediately. Turn upside down to drain on foil or wax paper. Allow to dry completely before each new coat is poured. After the lacquer begins to build up, drying may take a matter of hours. Don't rush it.

3. To decorate the exterior, rub a base coat of color or stain into the skin using furniture stain or acrylics applied with soft cloth. When color satisfies you, draw the design on the gourd with a pencil and fill it in with freehand strokes with the markers or acrylics. Finish by spraying with six coats of spray lacquer. Dry between coats.

Use the same materials and procedures as in preceding projects. This gourd is 5 inches across and
5 inches deep. The interior is natural.

OBSERVATIONS: This bowl was created as a gift
for friends so they would have a ceremonial bowl
in case they ever needed one. I designed it as
though it were a family portrait. There are trees,
sunshine, grass, children and animals all coming
down in harmony with the parents, John and
Barbara. Small ovular shapes, representing the spirit
of joy and hope that this family radiates, appear
along the lower edge of the bowl. On the under-
side are several running, closed lines to represent
the earth and its deep affection for this family.

CEREMONIAL BOWL
(Figure 55)

Use the same tools and materials as in preceding
projects except for the addition of 2 yards of
leather lacing, which forms the handle of the bag. I
used a leather shoelace from a shoe repair shop.
The gourd is 5 inches in diameter and 8 inches
long. The top 2 inches of the gourd were cut off
and after the bag was decorated, I drilled two sets
of holes on the sides. One set was 1½ inches down
from the top and one set 1 inch below that—four
on each side. I then threaded lacing through holes
to the length I wanted for handle, and tied the
thong in a knot. Chestnuts were added to one side
for decoration.

BEACH BAG (Figure 55)

CHRISTMAS ORNAMENTS
(Figure 56)

Materials and tools are the same, with the addition of wire, thread or yarn for hanging.

PROCEDURE

Decorate them any way you wish. Some of these had an undercoating of a product called Metallic Luster Wax. It comes in a nice variety of colors and is applied like paste wax. It adds both sheen and color. You can paint over it with acrylics and pens, but the label indicates it shouldn't be used on anything in which food will be served. I don't imagine many people eat out of their tree decorations, though.

To decorate the stained-glass globe (Figure 56, second row, left), I first cut off the bottom of gourd and then drilled random holes in it ⅛ inch in diameter. I painted it and then pushed cloves inside the holes with a drop of glue. Dyed squash seeds were then glued to surface.

To string the open-ended decorations, I drilled two holes at top of gourd ½ inch apart and pulled thread or wire through the holes.

Uncut spheres present more of a challenge. You can glue a length of decorative cord to the top of sphere. Make a little circle of the cord and glue this to the top, leaving enough to form a loop for hanging. Or you can drill two holes ½ inch apart opposite each other on bottom and top of gourd. Push a length of wire 12 inches long down through top hole and out the other side. Leave a 4-inch length outside the gourd. Turn the wire and come

FIGURE 56 *Christmas ornaments. Small garden gourds about the size of an orange are fun to decorate. Designs can be sketched on the woody surface with a pencil and then painted with acrylics and marking pens. This kind of gourd is very easy to grow. Only two vines will produce twenty or thirty gourds.*

back up through holes on other side. Twist the two ends together to form a hanging loop and cut off unneeded length.

For feather ornament (top), use two pieces that have been cut away from other gourds, one slightly smaller than the other:

1. Smooth edge of pieces with sandpaper; paint face on the smaller piece and spray both pieces with six coats of spray lacquer.

2. Drill ten holes at even intervals around the edge of the larger (back) piece, about ½ inch in from edge. The feathers will be pushed through these holes.

3. Push one or two feathers through each hole with quill ends meeting at the center. They now form a platform on which the face can be glued.

4. Squeeze ribbon of white glue in a circle over the feather ends. Lay face on this circle of glue and hold gently for a few minutes until the glue grabs the face.

5. When it is dry, thread a string for hanging through one of the top feather holes.

WIND CHIME (Figure 57) The hanging wind chime, which makes a shy little clatter when it moves, was made from one gourd 5 inches in diameter and three gourds 3 inches in diameter. Additional materials: Piece of yarn or cord 3 yards long, nine wooden beads.

FIGURE 57 *Left to right, wind chimes, dipper and birdhouse. The chimes were made by the author. Others were partially finished by Clara Comstock, an Oklahoma woman who grows lots of gourds and signs all her cards and letters with a "God love you."*

PROCEDURE

1. Following basic directions for cutting and preparing gourds, cut tops from all four gourds, remove seeds, and sand edges.

2. Rub outsides with stain and finish with spray lacquer. Insides are left natural.

3. Drill two holes in top of each gourd, ½ inch apart, for stringing on yarn.

4. Rub several drops of glue into each end of the yarn. This will harden the yarn and it will act as its own needle when you start to string. Start at the top with both ends and string them down through both holes in the largest gourd. Leave a 6-inch loop at the top for hanging. Tie a knot to hold the gourd at the bottom hole.

5. String one bead on each length just under the gourd and tie a knot under it to hold bead in place.

6. Continue to string gourds and beads in this fashion, following illustration (Figure 57). Join the two lengths of yarn at the bottom of hanging, and string one bead over the two lengths. Decorate with feathers or fray ends of yarn. Cut off what isn't needed.

BIRDHOUSE (Figure 57)

Clara cut the door in the house before she sent it to me. I sanded it and added three coats of paste wax to the exterior. Some bird-lovers hang a half-dozen houses together to provide communes for commune-type birds. Purple martins love them. Wrens won't go near them.

Clara cut this gourd too; I gave it the rocks to hold when it hangs outside; the wind makes it turn back and forth and keeps putting the rocks to sleep.

People have used gourds to make music almost as long as people and gourds have shared the earth. The spherical shape and woody skin make them ideal resonating chambers. In Africa an animal skin was stretched over a hole cut in the top and they became drums. They have also been hung on the plucking string of an instrument called a mouth bow. Gourd instruments called cabacas and maracas were used to produce a rattling sound; and another, the guiro, was a long cylindrical gourd with grooves cut on one side. It was played by scratching it with a stick. I didn't see the photograph myself, but there was a picture in *Life* magazine a few years ago that showed Pablo Casals at the age of six playing a one-string cello his father had fashioned from a gourd.

1. Cut top off gourd and finish as in general directions, pages 124–25.

2. I used a skin drumhead purchased from a music store, but a head can be cut from a piece of rawhide too. Soak the skin until it feels very pliant and then punch holes all around its edge, about 1 inch in from the edge and 2 inches apart. A paper punch will work if you don't have a leather punch.

DIPPER (Figure 57)

DRUM (Figure 58)

FIGURE 58 *Drum and bowl cut from gourds purchased at a folk fair in Mountain View, Arkansas. The lady who sold them whispered that the largest one was pregnant. "It will give you dozens of gourds next summer," she said.*

PROCEDURE

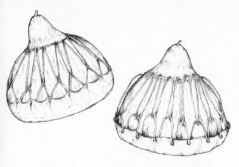

FIGURE 59 *Commercial drumhead forms the top of this gourd drum. At left, the head is drawn up so it is taut. The figure at the right indicates what it looks like as it is being laced.*

BIG MOUTH BOWL (Figure 58)

3. While the skin is still wet, lay it over top of the gourd and attach it by lacing it down with strong cord. (See Figure 59.) Other lacing designs can be used.

4. After it is all laced loosely, pull the lacings in tight to make sure the skin is taut. It will shrink as it dries and pull up a bit more.

5. Decorate the head after it has dried. You can leave a few seeds in so it will rattle when it is being drummed.

This gourd was 6 inches in diameter. It was prepared the same way as the preceding gourds. The interior was left natural.

PROCEDURE

1. Draw opening in gourd with pencil. Score along this line with a knife until you have gradually cut through the skin. Or drill holes at several places along the line and then enlarge one of the holes until you can insert just the blade from a coping saw. Using a gentle, almost featherlike stroke, saw along the pencil line.

2. Decorate with paints and pens.

3. Finish with six coats of lacquer.

SOME THOUGHTS ABOUT GROWING YOUR OWN GOURDS

In the Sources of Supplies and Information, I've listed places you can write for information about buying gourds and seeds. Gourds are quite easy to grow and need only sunshine and something on which to climb. The nice thing about growing your own is that they can be shaped as they grow. What you do is wait until they begin to assume a definite form and then alter it by wrapping it with cloth or yarn. Some people have had success growing them inside a box. You *do* have to be gentle, though. A gourd will only take so much manipulating and then it will fight back.

I haven't tried growing gourds in the house yet, but I see no reason why it can't be done. After the seed has sprouted and begins to look like a vine, set it in a sunny window and give it something to climb on. Stand back, though, for they grow quickly and the vines are thick and heavy with leaves. The only problem in growing them inside is that they need to be pollinated. So unless you have a crew of bees you can bring in, you'll have to do the job yourself. Take a paint brush and gather pollen from the flowers on the soft bristles of the brush. Go over all the flowers, "painting" them with pollen. You probably should do this several days in a row to be sure none of them are missed. Even if they don't produce fruit, the blossoms are beautiful.

EARTH WALKERS

Good Used Animal Parts

To NATIVE AMERICANS, the deer was a walking variety store. But, then, so were the buffalo, fish, moose, rabbit, porcupine and all other creatures that shared the earth. Animals represented a source of food, clothing, shelter, pots and most of the tools needed to make those things with. They were even a source for music-making materials and ornaments for the body. Every part of the animal seems to have been used—right down to the teeth and toenails. And fine material it was to work with too. You can't beat the combined toughness and malleability of rawhide. Or the self-threading efficiency and beauty of porcupine quills. What single raw material could you find today that would make a rattle, bowl, spoon, purse, drinking mug and wrench? Antler would do it. And so would shoulder blades, femur and tibia. It seems Indians were excellent ecologists before it became popular to be one.

When examining some of these cups and pots—in other words, the everyday "things" of the past—it's sometimes difficult to determine whether their ultimate goal was to be an object of utility or a work of art. Of course this isn't universally true, but it's true in enough cases to be provocative. Decorative work was intimate, often spectacular, and represented hours, days, even months of work. I don't think this necessarily meant that men and women had so little to do that they could sit idly around and stitch hundreds of two-inch-long porcupine quills to a piece of skin. I like to think, rather, that the person felt the spirituality inherent in the material and enjoyed spending time with it. He was at peace with the tusk he carved or the bone he engraved. Why should he hurry on to something else? Art, religion, food, life in general, were all so solidly integrated that a man choosing a material to make a war club, a flute or a robe would consider it only normal to select something with the "right" spirit. That's why we read about war whistles being made from the bones of a whooping crane, a bird that was extremely difficult to kill. Or necklaces being made

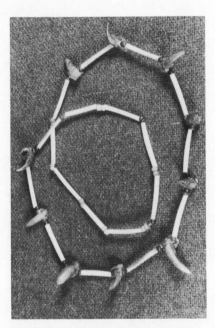

FIGURE 60 *Necklace made of otter claws, collection of First People, Chicago.*

from the claws of the grizzly bear, which was respected for its strength and courage. There is, fortunately, a growing interest in this kind of art, and it can be seen not only in museums but also in a number of small shops around the country. One example is First People in Chicago, a gallery-like operation that displays and sells the art and craft work of native Americans. The owners have a knowledgeable collection that includes whalebone carvings, feather bonnets, claw necklaces, and so on (Figure 60).

Jewelry, Music and Art from Bones

Every material formed by nature seems to be fickle, freckled, various and, best of all, unified by its variety. Bone is no exception. Bone is dense but it is porous too. Bones are flat, but they're also round. They're long, short, ridged and smooth. A friend of mine once found a moose bone on a camping trip. A pelvic bone it was, bleached white and curving around a natural, smooth center hole. She brought it home and mounted it on a black metal rod, and when you sit at her grand piano you can look through that hole right out across a big lake. It's a structurally beautiful piece of sculpture. It doesn't matter that people who see it assume that's what it is rather than a piece of bone that once connected a hip to a leg.

SOURCES AND CHOICES OF MATERIAL

In the arid parts of the western United States, I'm told that interesting bones can be picked up from the desert floor all shiny clean and polished by the elements. That's really nice. And as a midwesterner I'm envious. But bones are available from the supermarket too—those you get without asking whenever you buy a leg of lamb, a soup bone or a chicken. And the kind you can also get for nothing if you have the courage to ask. The butcher I asked was super-polite and gave me so many bones I couldn't lift the box. It was almost too heavy for him too, but that's because he was laughing so hard at my statement that I intended to make jewelry from them. I would have been embarrassed if I hadn't been so pleased with this good present.

Save any bones that look intriguing from anything you serve. A ham bone is hollow and has a slight exterior twist. Chicken vertebrae look like miniature sculptured beads. There are no two exactly alike, and they come with a natural hole for stringing. Leg bones from turkey, chicken or any fowl can be cut into long beads or shaped into whistles. The pelvic bone of a chicken is a natural pendant.

What you're likely to get from the butcher are the long bones that are cut away when he prepares boneless rolled roasts of beef, ham or lamb.

Ask for a doggie bag if you are served frog legs in a restaurant. They are ivory-colored hollow stems.

PREPARATION NOTES

Bones have to be cleaned very soon after you bring them home or they will make you feel unhappy to be near them. Drop them into a big pot as though you were going to make soup. Add a bit of detergent and simmer until the extraneous tissue can be scrubbed away. Times vary with the size of the bone, but a very large one might take as long as three hours. A chicken bone needs only half an hour. The soft marrow should be removed too. It will come out with a bottle brush.

Bones can be bleached by placing them overnight (after they are clean) in a pot to which ammonia has been added. Use one-half cup to a gallon of water. In the morning, rinse away ammonia water and set the bones aside to dry.

A very helpful anthropologist from the Smithsonian says that burying bones in dirt (a window box will do) for one to two weeks will remove organic materials from them and leave them in a pristine condition. If you live someplace where there are ants, and it's summertime, you can leave bones out for the ants to find. They'll gladly clean them for you. Several knowledgeable people have told me this really works. I've not tried it myself, but it sounds legitimate if you want to give it a whirl.

Hacksaw, drill with a 1/16" and 1/8" bit, a mill file (this is a file with a flat surface), a rattail file, No. 200 and No. 400 wet and dry paper, paste wax, spray lacquer.

To make the pendant (center) you will want a section of ham bone approximately 3 inches long. This one arrived that length in a picnic ham. In addition to the basic materials, above, you will also want a can of walnut furniture stain and a length of cord for hanging the pendant.

SIMPLE PENDANT (Frontispiece)

1. Smooth ends. Lay the file on table and rub the bone ends over it until they feel smooth. Smooth interior with the rattail file.

PROCEDURE

2. Drill six holes partially through the bone in a random design.

3. Using No. 200 wet and dry paper, polish pendant until it feels smooth. Switch to No. 400 paper and continue to polish until it feels like glass. Dip paper in water frequently as you work.

4. Spray on stain, rub into drilled holes, and then wipe away with a soft cloth. Finish with three coats of paste wax, allowing each to dry before applying next. Buff between each coat.

5. If bone does not have a natural bridge for the cord, drill two holes through top for this purpose.

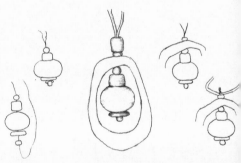

FIGURE 61 *Large figure at center is the beaded pendant. Around it, beginning at left, are the steps in stringing the beads inside the pendant.*

PENDANT WITH BEADS
(Frontispiece, right)
ADDITIONAL MATERIALS

In addition to the basic materials, page 142, you will want a spool of bead wire, six assorted beads, and two lengths of neck cord 13″ long. The one here is a silver satin cord purchased in a drapery shop.

PROCEDURE

1. Select a section of round, hollow bone approximately ½″ thick and 1½″ in diameter. Or saw one from a longer bone using a hacksaw.

2. Drill one hole with ⅛″ bit through top of bone.

3. Smooth all surfaces by rubbing first on the file and then using wet and dry paper. Lay a sheet of the No. 200 paper in bottom of a flat pan and cover it with 2″ of water. Rub bone over the paper (right in the water) and when it is smooth, switch to No. 400 paper to give it a high gloss.

4. String beads and hang through hole (Figure 61). Run a 6″ length of bead wire down through hole and place five beads on it (or the number that will fit). Run wire around last bead and back up through the other beads and out through the top.

5. Take ends of wire through one small bead; leave a loop and then tie in several knots. Run neck cord through loop and bring one large bead down over cord to cover knots and loop.

PENDANT WITH LEATHER TRIM *(Frontispiece, left)*

A single-edged razor blade, rubber cement, scraps of leather—one piece ⅛″ thick, ½″ wide, and 6″ to 8″ long; one piece of soft, thin leather about

3″x 5″, and one length of thong 34″ long for neck cord; a bright feather.

1. Select a hollow bone ½″ thick and 1½″ to 2″ in diameter. Smooth and polish as in directions for pendant with beads, above. You don't have to polish sides of bone that will be covered with leather.

2. Cut a scrap of leather to line the inside hole of bone. Following directions on label of rubber cement, place leather trim in hole, pat it firmly in place, and trim away any excess after it dries.

3. Cut strip of leather for exterior of bone. Measure around outside of bone to determine proper length; add 3″ and then mark cutting line. (To cut leather, lay it on a firm board and place a metal ruler on the cutting line. Cut with a razor blade.)

4. Prepare neck thong. Reduce thickness of the last inch of both ends of the thong by shaving away about ¼″ with razor blade (Figure 62). Place thinned ends together and glue. Wrap with rubber bands till dry.

5. Coat outer surface of bone and surface of leather wrapping with rubber cement. Align bone, thong and leather wrapping, and press into place (Figure 63).

6. Wrap whole assembly with string and let dry. Then cut strips of thin leather and wrap around top of pendant. Put a bright feather in with the wrapping. Glue ends in place.

ADDITIONAL MATERIALS

PROCEDURE

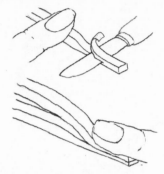

FIGURE 62   *Thinning the last inch of both ends of thong.*

FIGURE 63   *Left to right, placing thong between leather wrapping; pendant after wrapping is glued and bound; pendant before being bound.*

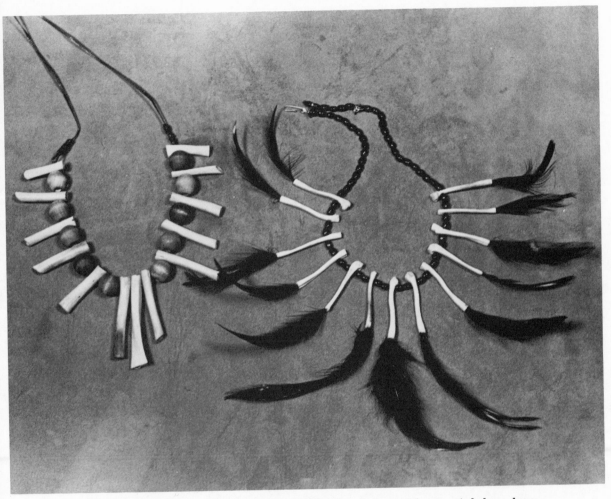

FIGURE 64   *Necklace at left is made of chicken bones with one pink ham bone at the center. The varicolored wooden beads are remnants of a child's old game. Frog bones, right, are smooth and ivory colored. Beads and feathers are a crisp glossy black.*

In addition to the basic materials, page 142, you will need an assortment of chicken leg bones, a small ham bone, two lengths of thin leather lacing 4″ long, one spool of bead wire, assorted beads, and 1 yard of satin cordage from a drapery shop.

1. Saw ends from leg bones and simmer to make them fresh and sweet. Clean out softened marrow and tissue. This necklace contains one small ham bone and twelve chicken bones, but prepare more than you need. Some will break when they're sawed.

2. Smooth cut ends with a file and No. 200 wet and dry paper.

3. Drill holes at top end of each bone for stringing. Use $\frac{1}{16}$″ bit.

4. String bones and beads on wire, using illustration as a guide for design. Or use one of your own.

5. Make a loop at each end of wire by running ends of wire back through last two beads and tying in a knot (Figure 65, top).

6. Cut two 12″ lengths of cord and bring ends through wire loop and back out to cord (Figure 65, middle). Glue ends to cord and wrap with a 4″ strip of leather lacing. Glue ends in place (Figure 65, bottom).

This necklace was made by drilling holes in twelve frog leg bones after they were cleaned. Feathers were pulled out of an old hat from a thrift shop.

BEADS AND BARE BONES
(Figure 64, left)
ADDITIONAL MATERIALS

PROCEDURE

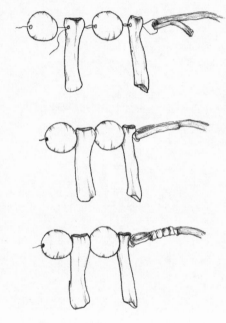

FIGURE 65 *Steps in stringing bone and bead necklace.*

BONE AND FEATHER NECKLACE *(Figure 64, right)*

Since the bones were hollow, it was easy to place a drop of glue on each feather and push it up inside the bones. Shiny black beads were purchased from a craft shop. Necklace was assembled on bead wire.

CHICKEN VERTEBRAE AND BEAD NECKLACE (Figure 66)
ADDITIONAL MATERIALS

You will need a bowl of chicken vertebrae—this necklace contains sixty-two; one batch of tiny glass beads and two large beads. You will also need two bottles of Glass Stain, a product available in craft shops. I used Ruby Red and Amber.

PROCEDURE

1. Simmer and scrub bones.

2. Pour Glass Stain into two small tin cans and pour thirty-six bones into the red, twenty-six into the amber. Stir until well coated. Spread out to dry.

3. Repeat process three times or until bones have picked up sufficient color. Dry. Spray with three coats of lacquer.

4. String on bead wire, alternating colors as you wish. Place three tiny glass beads between each bone bead. Tie knot in end of string and drop on a dot of glue.

BONE WHISTLES (Figure 66)

A variety of rhythm instruments has been made from animal parts. Steer horns, deer hooves, bird claws, bits of bones and even cocoons were once strung on rawhide strips to make rattling sounds for dances. Sometimes a whole tortoise or turtle

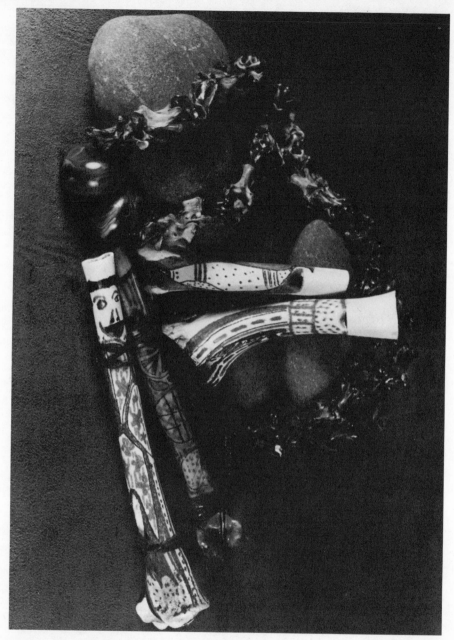

FIGURE 66   Necklace of chicken vertebrae with two large beads, and selection of decorated toy whistles made of turkey and chicken leg bones. The colors are bright and they can be either worn around the neck or hung on the Christmas tree.

shell became a rattle too, which was worn just above the knee. The jawbones of horses and mules, complete with their teeth, also made rhythm instruments. After it was mounted on something or just held in the hand, a stick was scraped back and forth over the teeth. Beautiful flutes and whistles were made from bone—mostly the long bones of birds, which were decorated with carvings. A very simple whistle can be made from a turkey leg bone and hung around the neck or on the Christmas tree.

ADDITIONAL MATERIALS

In addition to the basic materials, you will need one turkey leg bone (or one from a long-legged chicken) for each whistle. To decorate them you might want scraps of leather lacing, beads, feathers and marking pens. You will also need a cord to hang them.

PROCEDURE

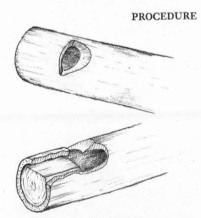

1. Saw off small end of bone and clean (see page 141).

2. Make a triangular cut with a coping saw on top side, 1″ from end of bone (Figure 67).

3. Make a plug for mouthpiece by whittling a piece of soft wood to fit the inside circumference of bone, and long enough to reach the cut.

4. Remove plug and whittle away top so it is flat. Push back in bone and jiggle and trim until you have a good fit. Blow across till you get the tone you want.

FIGURE 67 *The triangular cut, top. Bottom, a cut-away view showing the "plug" in place.*

5. Decorate with markers, beads, feathers, etc. Tie on a lacing.

In addition to the basic materials, you will need one can of white mat finish enamel, one piece of masonite or hardwood measuring 12″ x 18″, white glue, selection of beef bones.

To make this painting, the artist cut some bones and selected others from the collection he had on hand. One end of the bone was polished till it glistened (see page 143.) A design was worked out first on paper, and then the bones were attached to the board with white glue after it had been sprayed with two coats of paint.

NOTE: For information on where to find feathers and leather scraps and lacings for jewelry in this chapter, see pages 192–94.

Except for bones, which start out inside where it's warm and cozy, leather comes closest to being a very real, almost oxygen-breathing material. It speaks of its animalness in a variety of sensuous ways. It feels good when you touch it, smells delicious, and looks rich and lush. It's also malleable without being disgustingly servile.

In fact, when I consider the number of processes and hours involved in changing an animal hide into something else, I'm overwhelmed at the skill

BONE PAINTING (Figure 68)
ADDITIONAL MATERIALS

PROCEDURE

FIGURE 68 *Polished lengths of bone are mounted on a board in an all-white "painting." The interior surface of the bones is rough and delicately tinted with shades of brown.*

Skin

and patience of native craftsmen. The beautiful embroidered sheepskin coats that are imported from Persia (Iran) today require hours, days, weeks, months just to prepare the skin for cutting. Over a period of time it gets salted down, dried in the sun, driven to the river on the back of a mule, washed, stretched, salted again and then rubbed with oil and pomegranate rind. After all that, the hide is turned over and the fleece side is attended to.

The highly decorated buckskin shirts, tipis and parfleches of the American Indian are no less impressive. Starting out with a furry animal hide, the leather worker first had to get rid of the unwanted fat and fur. He had a number of options, but none of them was quick or easy. All required the cooperation of nature. The hide could be stretched on the earth so the insects could work it over; it could be buried in dirt so the earth could do its job, or it could be staked out in a running stream so the water could have a go at it. After this initial softening process, it was ready to be fleshed (scraped) with tools of bone or flint. Then, after intermittent bouts of stretching, washing and drying, it was rubbed down with a soothing paste made from the brains of a deer. If it was going to be a piece of rawhide, the process stopped there; if not, it had to be smoked over a slow-burning fire. Of course all these efforts preceded the decorating processes. Depending on the nature of their intended use, the hides were dyed, painted, beaded or embroidered with quills.

SOME KINDS OF LEATHER AND SOURCES

Speaking very broadly, leather for craft purposes falls into two categories—tooling leather, which is thick enough to carve, and garment leather, which is not. Garment leather can be handled like cloth in that it can be stitched on an ordinary sewing machine, cut with scissors, etc. An extremely thin version of garment leather is called skiver. Skin treated in this way is used for lining boxes, gloves and purses (and sometimes secret pockets). The terms "lacing" and "thong" are confusing because they are often used interchangeably In this chapter, though, "thong" will signify a heavy leather at least one-eighth inch thick, while "lacing" will indicate a thinner, more flexible material.

There are leather and skin shops listed in the yellow pages of your telephone directory, and it may be worth a trip to one of them if you don't know much about leather and want to learn. Craft and hardware stores often sell remnant or scrap bundles of leather too. Pieces are usually packaged by the pound and divided into either garment or tooling bundles. Mail-order sources are listed in the Sources of Supplies and Information.

FIGURE 69 *Leather choker is a rosy brown with gold braid at its edge. The cowrie shells are an off-white with rings of brown encircling patches of blue. The shells are as smooth as satin.*

Paper punch with a round hole, scissors, one spool of gold metallic thread, one package of gold soutache braid, one package of drilled cowrie shells, one remnant of garment leather large enough to provide a piece 1½" wide by 9" long.

1. Measure out dimensions of choker on paper and tape to back side of leather to hold it in place while you cut.

2. Find center of choker and stitch six large shells to lower edge—three on each side of the center. Use metallic thread. Arrange them so they don't quite touch. Run thread through holes in shell two times. Tie off thread at end (Figure 70).

3. Thread two strings of shells 4" long, two strings 11" long and one string 15" long. Cut thread twice as long as you need for finished length —that is, for the 4" length allow 8". To thread, take thread through hole in cowrie shell two times and then tie in a knot before tying on the next shell (Figure 71). Do not cut thread between shells. Attach each cowrie so it hangs with approximately ¾" of space between it and the previous one. After last one is strung, tie a final knot and place a drop of glue on knot. Cut off extra thread.

4. Sew strings of shells to choker between the original large shells. Put the longest string in the middle, the shortest on the outside, etc.

5. Outline choker with soutache braid by stitching it to leather with a simple running stitch.

SHELL AND LEATHER CHOKER *(Figure 69)*

MATERIALS AND EQUIPMENT

PROCEDURE

FIGURE 70 *Shells attached to leather.*

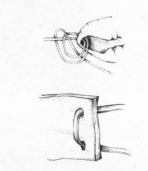

FIGURE 71 *Top, knotting the cowrie shell to the cord. Below, attaching soutache ties to choker*

6. Punch two holes at each end of choker, ½″ in from end. Cut two pieces of soutache 12″ long and lace through holes (Figure 71).

EXTRA POCKETS (Figure 72)
MATERIALS AND EQUIPMENT

Scissors, colorful scraps of fabric with a design that can be cut out, small vial of colorful beads, felt-tipped markers (NOTE: I like to use markers called Dri-Mark), one 44″ length of thong for shoulder strap (for each pocket), one package of garment leather remnants, small mirrors (1½″ to 2″), rubber cement.

PROCEDURE

1. Make a pattern for pockets on a sheet of plain paper (Figure 73).
2. Cut out paper pattern and secure it to back side of leather with clear tape. Cut out.
3. Fold loop (C) in the middle and lay just below fold line of pocket (A), with folded end facing toward center and other ends lining up with edges of pocket (Figure 74).
4. Stitch pocket together on sewing machine by laying section (B) over lower half of (A). Catch loops at the same time. Turn stitching to inside.

DECORATING THE POCKETS

Pocket, far left, Figure 72: Cut an appropriate design from a piece of fairly lightweight fabric. Place on leather, and outline design area with a pencil. Then coat both the back of the cloth and the

FIGURE 72 *Extra pockets (to hold anything special) are cut from remnants of soft, pale brown leather and decorated with bright fabric, glass beads and markers. Under each flap is a small mirror.*

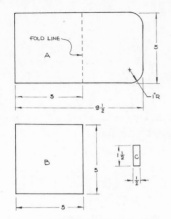

FIGURE 73 *Pattern for pockets.*

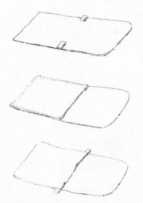

FIGURE 74 *Assembling the pocket: Top, loops laid in place; center, B laid over A and stitched; bottom, stitching turned to inside.*

marked-off design area with rubber cement. Press together and allow to dry. Coat back of small mirror and center of design with rubber cement and press together. Optional: Outline flap and design with markers. Attach shoulder strap.

Pocket, above right, Figure 72: Outline edge of flap with marker. Create your own design or start out with a variation of this one by making main part, or V shape, with ruler. Lay ruler on flap and draw alongside with markers. Add dots, swirls, etc., in freehand.

Pocket, lower right, Figure 72: Cut an appropriate design from fabric and glue to leather with rubber cement. Outline design with delicate beads that have been strung on bead thread. Place a string of beads along the edge of the design and, using a needle and thread, sew to leather with overhand stitches (Figure 75). Make a stitch over every third bead and down through leather.

Rawhide. Rawhide is a fascinating material to work with, though you might be turned off by it at first. It is pale, stiff and greasy looking, but after being soaked in water it becomes pliant and soft. It dries to a smooth, hard surface that is fun to decorate. The Plains Indians made and decorated beautiful shields from extra-thick rawhide—thick and tough enough to turn aside arrows. Boxes, purses, and containers for food were also made of this material and then painted with geometric designs. But rawhide was, and still could be, a material almost perfectly suited to anything requiring a stout binding. It was used effectively to lash stones to pieces of bone or wood for tools, and also for nets, snowshoes and hoops. Lashed or sewn while wet, it shrank as it dried to form a perfect, unbreakable bond.

Making Things from Rawhide. Rawhide is available from the same sources as garment leather (see Sources of Supplies and Information). Normally it is made from goat or calf and is sold by the whole skin.

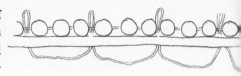

FIGURE 75 *Method of stitching beads to pocket.*

A drill with ⅛″ bit, paper punch with a round hole, scissors, tom-tom frame measuring 3″ high and 12″ in diameter, one piece of rawhide large enough to provide a circle 16″ in diameter. You will also want 5 yards of ¼″ wide rawhide lacing, a 12″ dowel and marking pens to decorate the head. NOTE: If you like, you can order a rawhide tom-tom head and not bother cutting one yourself. For a 12″ frame, order a 15″ or 16″ head. The extra width is for material that needs to be stretched down over the sides of the frame. Heads come in sizes from 8″ to 30″ in diameter. The heads, frame, lacing, pens, etc., are available from Grey Owl. See Sources of Supplies and Information.

TOM-TOM

MATERIALS AND TOOLS

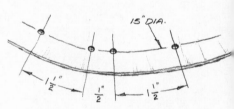

FIGURE 76: (*a*) *Laying out a circle 16 inches diameter.* (*b*) *Holes punched ½ inch in from edge.*

1. Lay out skin and mark off a circle 16″ in diameter (Figure 76a). Cut out circle with scissors.

PROCEDURE

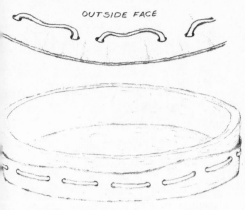

OUTSIDE FACE

2. Mark holes for punching ½″ in from edge, or on a 15″ diameter circle (Figure 76b). Alternate holes in this fashion: ½″, 1½″, ½″, 1½″, etc.

3. Punch holes as marked.

4. Soak skin and lacing for three or four hours. It becomes transparent looking and feels supple and smooth when it's ready. (It wouldn't hurt to soak it overnight.)

5. Begin to lace head by taking lacing through holes so the 1½″ span of lace will be on the outside of the head (Figure 77a).

6. Lay head face-down on table and place frame in the center of head. Pull head up around frame as you tighten lace. Pull lace up snug and tie (Figure 77b).

7. Tie a new lace to one of the 1½″ segments of secured lace (Figure 78). Lace head by taking this lacing across bottom of drum and picking up the 1½″ segment of lacing directly opposite. Go back and forth in this fashion, pulling lace and head as tight as possible until head is laced. (The skin will shrink as it dries.) End of lace will be tied to starting segment. Tie securely.

8. Where laces cross at the center, tie on a new strand. Weave this strand in and out of the crossed laces as tightly as possible. This forms a ball-like grouping that makes a hand grip.

9. When head is dry, decide on a design and mark it on with a pencil. Paint with felt-tipped markers (be sure to use waterproof ones).

FIGURE 77: (*a*) *Lacing.* (*b*) *Fitting head to bottom.*

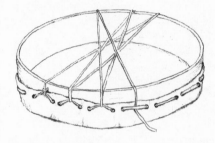

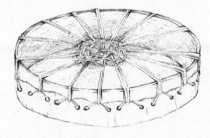

FIGURE 78 *Lacing head, top. Completed lacing, bottom.*

10. Make a "beater" by wrapping scraps of leather around one end of a 12″ dowel.

One tom-tom frame 3″ high and 12″ in diameter, 10 yards of ¼″ rawhide lacing, electric drill with ⅛″ bit, spray enamel, undercoating paint, sandpaper.

1. Make a paper pattern as follows: An 8½″ square fits inside a 12″ circle (Figure 80). With this as a start, divide the square into 1¹⁄₁₆″ segments. The holes will be drilled in the frame where the lines cross the circle.

2. Lay out the holes by laying the frame on the pattern and marking edge of frame according to pattern.

3. Mark a line all around frame ½″ from bottom.

4. Transfer edge marks to this line.

5. Drill ⅛″ holes on intersection of marks.

6. Sand frame until smooth, spray with undercoat, sand, and apply two coats of enamel. Dry thoroughly.

7. Soak lacing three or four hours. Tie knot in one end and lace tray in a checkerboard pattern. Keep lacing taut and firm as you go. Tie knot at end.

WOOD AND RAWHIDE BASKET *(Figure 79)*
MATERIALS AND TOOLS

PROCEDURE

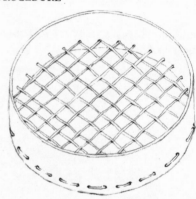

FIGURE 79 *Rawhide basket with wooden frame. The frame is a bright glossy red enamel. The strips of rawhide are pale brown and have an organic-looking texture that contrasts nicely with the sleek red frame.*

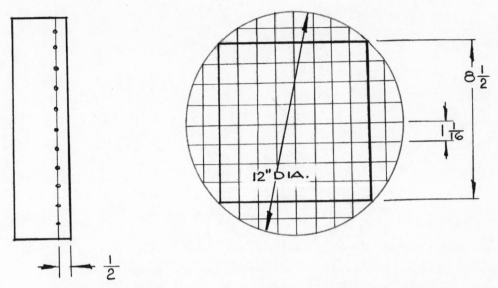

FIGURE 80   *Method of laying out a pattern for drilling holes in frame.*

FLYERS, SWIMMERS, FALLERS & OTHER SMALL PERFORMING ARTISTS

Two Fallers   RAIN AND SNOW fall freely on us all and, as improbable as it may sound, there are ways of passing them on to someone as a present. You don't even have to stretch a point to do it. A jug of rain water wouldn't make a bad gift at all—for a dyer, a gardener, someone about to wash her hair, or a good soul who would just be enchanted to have a private collection of rain water. Dyers welcome rain because it's a pristine carrier for their dye solutions. Without it they might have to buy distilled water. And anyone who has ever shampooed her hair in rain water knows what a shiny trip *that* is! I'm surprised some entrepreneur hasn't started bottling it for sale. As for gardeners (both indoors and out), they claim that melted snow and rain are superior natural fertilizers because they contain large amounts of nitrogen. Getting nitrogen into the soil is a feat most gardeners have to pay to achieve.

Capturing rain requires only a rainfall and a large container to set under a rainspout. If there's no such spout on the corner of your house, just set a tub out under the sky. It won't collect there quite so quickly, nor in such volume, but it will work. A generation or so ago, every well-appointed home of any size had a cistern for catching and storing rain. If it didn't have a cistern, it at least had a rain barrel to catch the runoff from the roof. It wasn't a matter of economy or convenience either. Rain was really treasured for its special softness. There's a mansion in my small town with a gigantic cistern built into a third-floor attic room. A fair-sized elephant could bathe there with pleasure if he could get up the winding stairs. Obviously the owner of this home saved more rain water than most people.

It's too bad no one has ever figured out a way to save snow. For the most part, people start getting rid of it the minute it falls. They do in the cities anyway, for snow and automobiles don't marry well at all. Sad, because snow lays down a clean white cover over dirty streets, abandoned wrecks, and used-car lots. I have to admit, though, that an accumulation of snow can cause problems. While one single flake on an Airedale's nose can be an esthetic delight, a bunch of them in one place can break tree branches and hide fire hydrants. As a matter of fact, if snow were left to its own devices, it would eventually become a glacier by virtue of its own weight and abundance.

Apart from all that, you can put snow to some very tasty uses. People who go out in the spring to gather sap from maple trees like to pour the sap, boiling hot, into clean white snow to create instant maple candy—cold, hot and sweet all at the same time. New Englanders call this confection "Leather Aprons." My grandmother and her peers used to mix handfuls of snow with sugar, vanilla and condensed milk to make a bucolic version of ice cream. If you want to try this sometime, take a can of condensed milk, one teaspoon of vanilla, and one cup of sugar. Put it in a bowl and keep adding one handful of snow after another until it looks and tastes a lot like ice cream. Add different fruits and flavors for variety.

Aside from these culinary treats, one thing about snow pleases me every time I consider it—the fact that snowflakes are crystals. The next time one falls on your sleeve or on the porch steps, whip out a magnifying glass and check it out. Keep the crystal image in your head for a while. It can't help but make you feel edified.

Sources for rain and snow: the sky.

Trees don't have to be cut down and sawed into boards to make objects of utility and beauty. With very little help from any of us, they produce acorns, pollen, apples, bark, olives, nuts, shade, supports for tire swings, leaves and branches. There is a fascinating book called *Survival Arts of the Primitive Paiutes* by Margaret M. Wheat, which describes the ways the Paiute Indians used year-old wands of the willow tree before it formed any branches. Willow wands provided the raw material for nearly every item of the Paiutes' household goods.

"From them she wove the tough little water jugs that she carried in her hand against thirst in the desert," the writer says. "From them she made cradles for the newborn infant, the hat that protected her head, the vessel in which she cooked, the bowl into which she served, and the tray on which she parched seeds, harvested berries, dried meats, cleaned nuts and roots, and with which she seined fish. From the willows she wove the beater with which she gleaned the seeds from the grasses, and the basket on which the seeds were collected. And finally, with these willows she made the basket in which she carried all the other baskets."

Since we don't have to depend on trees for baskets, hats and bowls today, we can afford to wait

Tree Fallers

for parts of the tree to fall to the ground before we take them home to look at. Branches and twigs, picked up from the ground, are illustrated in several places in this book. They do things like hold up mobiles of feathers or support hangings of pods, galls, etc. Small fist-thick branches with interesting twisted shapes make excellent background frames for weavings. Bright yarns can be wound in and around them in a spider-web kind of pattern something like the God Eyes, page 84. They can be suspended or picked up and held. Children love to do these small weavings (Figure 81). Driftwood, of course, is "found" art from the trees. Nothing needs to be done to it. Though people traditionally expect to find it only along the beach, twisted and bleached pieces can be found on the forest floor too. Look along the edges of swamps and rivers.

Sometimes branches with burls on them fall from the trees. Burls are beautiful by-products of a tree's unhappy encounter with a disease or a wound. When a tree gets hurt or is attacked by certain diseases, it reacts by forming a healing welt —a little like what our appendages do when they form calluses from shoveling or playing the guitar. These welts are tightly compacted circles of growth that veer around in unpredictable directions (Figure 82). Wilderness travelers used to saw them off the branches, whittle out the inner core, and then use them for drinking cups. Burls of larger dimensions made indestructible, incredibly beauti-

FIGURE 81 *Twig weavings. Twigs that fall from trees can be wrapped with yarn and twine. These are sketches of weavings made by ten-year-olds.*

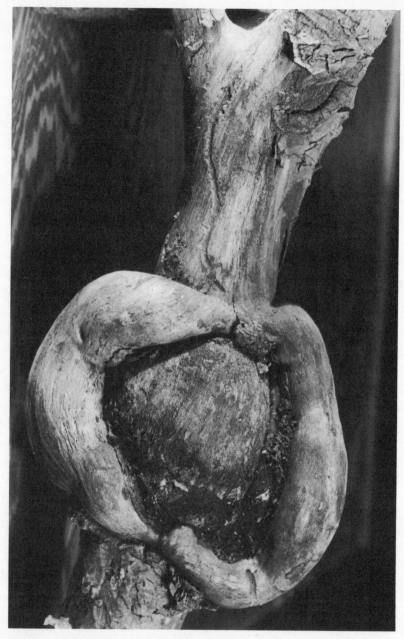

FIGURE 82 *A burl about 5 inches in diameter that has formed around a branch. Burls sometimes grow large enough to be made into bowls. They are works of natural art.*

ful bowls. In walks through the forest, you might come across a whole section of land where trees are decorated by burls. When the trees die, or the branches die and fall to the ground, the burls can be sawed off and carried home. They should never be cut from a growing tree.

One Small Artist— a Mushroom

Mushrooms have gills—or many kinds do, anyway. This means that if you turn one over you will see a cap filled with undulating ridges radiating from the stem to the cap's edge. Between these lines or ridges are millions of individually invisible spores, finer than dust. If you remove the stem and lay the cap face-down on a sheet of paper, the spores will fall out and create a beautiful print for you (Figure 83). (NOTE: Some mushrooms have spongy undersides. These will not work.) Take a sheet of watercolor paper, or one that has a fair amount of weight, and place it in a spot away from drafts. Better yet, after you place the mushroom, cover it with a bowl or box. The process takes a number of hours, though this varies so much with temperature and humidity that it's hard to pin down. Some people say it takes an overnight session, but I've found that four or five hours will do the trick. When you decide to check on it, lift the cap by the corner. Be extremely cautious because the design is dementedly fragile. If it's done, in other words if you see a design on the paper, lift

FIGURE 83 *Mushroom print. Three mushroom caps were laid down in an overlapping pattern and left to drop their spores on watercolor paper.*

the cap away entirely. Then, with even more cau-
tion and more bated breath, spray with lacquer.
Don't let me scare you too much, it's not all *that*
terrifying, but you do have to be careful if you
don't want to spoil the design. Hold the spray can
about three feet away and aim just above the paper
so the mist will fall *on* it rather than whoosh across
it. Wait five minutes and repeat. Then give it one
more spray for good measure. After spraying, the
paper can be handled like any other art print and
can be framed and mounted.

Sometimes I lay down a wash of watercolor first,
let it dry, and then arrange a group of mushrooms
of several sizes on the paper, some overlapping
the others.

Eggs, Large and Small

I wonder if any other natural object has ever
been decorated quite so extensively and with such
extravagance as the egg? This little thing has been
painted, waxed, dyed, glued, etched with acid,
cut open and had stuff pushed inside it, set on a
pedestal, had ribbons and jewels hung on it—the
list could go on. I suppose eggs like the treatment,
though, or they wouldn't continue to put up
with it.

People of almost every country, as far back as
we can go historically, have done their share of
egg decorating. My primary feeling is that eggs
don't really have to be decorated—except, of

FIGURE 84 *Eggs across the top are decorated with Tecnitape, while the ones in the box appear in their own natural beauty. (Courtesy of Rock Mountain Farm, Mosier, Oregon.) In the box are a dark green, shiny tinamou egg and a blue hen egg. The large one in the rear is from a turkey. (Plexiglass cube courtesy of Terra Cotta Potta, DeKalb, Illinois.)*

course, at Easter time when the Easter Bunny needs help. After all, eggs are considered to be nature's finest and purest design. But even as I write these words I'm preparing to offer a new decorating method to the ones already in use. It combines one of nature's oldest (or first) products with one of technology's newest. It's called Tecnitape and is used by people who do technical drawings —draftsmen, architects and designers. Tecnitape and similar products come in rolls of varying widths that are adhesive-backed. The narrowest is about a pencil-lead wide, or about $\frac{1}{32}$ inch. That's what makes it so delightful to work with. It's narrow enough to do curves by itself or to follow around the natural curve of an egg without wrinkling or buckling (Figure 84). There are also sheets of letters and numbers in a large variety of type styles. Old English lettering seems particularly provocative. There's no fuss or clean-up, and anything you don't like you can peel off and re-do. There are a large number of colors and a huge selection of designs. These tapes are sold in stationery and office-supply stores.

When eggs are being prepared for decoration, it is traditional either to boil them first or to remove their contents through holes punched in the shells. If you're going to do the latter, here's how it works: Take a needle and prick a hole in one end of an egg. I guess I don't have to tell you to do this very gingerly. Now prick a hole in the other end, but enlarge this one with a series of small holes until it is about the size of a pearl. Keep it as small as you can, but remember that everything inside that egg has to work its way out through the hole you make for it. Now, press your mouth against the small hole and blow steadily. It's a slow job so don't plan on doing a dozen or so at a time.

Because I hated to force the liquid contents out of eggs, I inadvertently discovered that this step could be eliminated. I just set eggs aside and let them rest in peace until they dehydrated. It takes a long time, but they require no attention so it doesn't matter. Quail eggs felt light and feathery at the end of nine months, but I can't honestly tell you how long it would take for an egg from a chicken or duck.

Sources. Eggs from chickens, since they're plentiful, are the ones most often used for decorating. (This, of course, discounts the plastic ones that are sold everyplace today.) However, duck and goose eggs are easy to find. They're larger and more fun to handle. Check the farm ads in the paper beginning in the spring months. In the Midwest, eggs are advertised beginning in late March, and the supply continues for six months. A hatchery is a source too. They are only interested in fertile eggs and will sell the others to craftsmen. Check the yellow pages under Poultry or Hatchery.

Exotic or unusual eggs that don't need (and shouldn't have) decorations are a little harder to come by but certainly worth the effort to find. Even brown chicken eggs have a special warmth and beauty. But did you know there are chickens (Araucanas) that lay eggs that are blue, pink and green? Or ducks that lay black eggs? And charcoal-colored ones? And blue? Then there's the egg of the tinamou bird, which is a beautiful chartreuse and has a shell as glossy as fine china. Button quail eggs are spackled with greens and blues, while a black Australian swan produces a pale green-blue egg. Exotic eggs like these are available from Rock Mountain Farm, Box 167, Mosier, Oregon 97040. There is a ten-cent price list. Ostrich and goose eggs can be ordered from Kathryn Johnson, Bushkill Drive, R.D. 2, Easton, Pennsylvania 18042. Write for prices.

Some Swimmers

I recently played a solitary game of trying to figure out a way to describe sea shells to someone who'd neither seen nor heard of them. After an hour or so of forming and rejecting explanations, I gave up and looked to see what the dictionary had to offer. The explanation disappointed me because of its simplicity: "a hard outer covering of an animal." I had thought it might describe a shell's formal, almost virginal beauty or lay a few words on me about its thousands of variations in

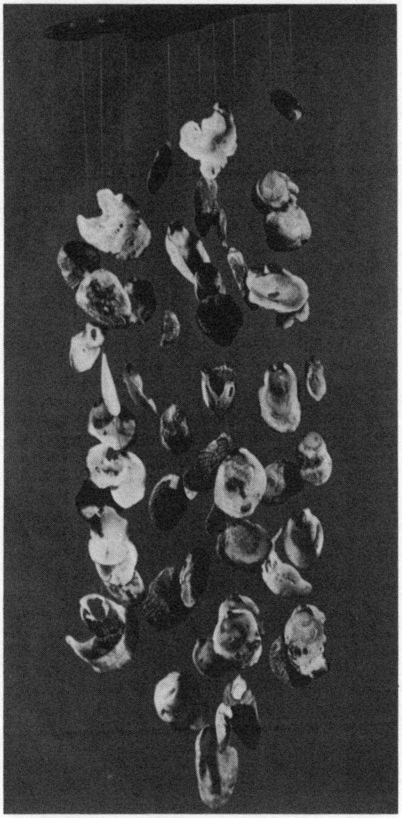

FIGURE 85 *Shell hanging is surprisingly sturdy. The individual strings hang from a branch and make a nice sound when they brush together. (Courtesy Brouhaha, De Kalb.)*

SHELL HANGING (Figure 85)

color and shape. Instead what it said, in effect, was that shells are mobile homes for marine life. So be it. That's a good thought too.

Some people collect and treasure shells in the same way that rock hounds pursue precious stones and rocks. They join clubs, have auctions, trades and sales, build special display cabinets, and become very serious indeed about their pursuit. To demonstrate how seriously shells can be regarded, they've been stolen from displays in museums. I guess this gives them the same prestige as paintings and sculpture.

Though some single shells are worth thousands of dollars, the kinds we are using in the following projects are far less prestigious numbers. Some are ordinary clam shells that can be gathered from the muddy edges of rivers and creeks. Others are the kind that get picked up on weekend trips to the shore—those that are given an honored place for several weeks after their trip from the ocean and then wind up in a cardboard box along with broken floor tiles, some splayed twine, and two bent bicycle spokes. But because they've spent time in the basement doesn't mean they're not worthy of attention. It's good to bring them out in the open where their beauty can shine.

If you'd like to make a shell hanging, look over your collection and drill one hole in the shells you want to use. (Shells are tough. It takes a long time to drill through.) String them on heavy fishing line and tie them to a branch. Use the same system of tying as that of the cowrie-shell necklace, page 154. A whole doorway can be filled by using strings of shells too. Put up a rod in the doorway and add one string of shells at a time until it is filled to your satisfaction. It's better to stick to fairly small shells. Large ones look handsome but add too much weight. These door hangings make such a good sound when someone passes through.

Clam shells make interesting tiny gardens. To make a cactus garden, buy the smallest variety of cactus the plant store carries. Some of them are only an inch high when they're fully grown. Place a drop of white glue in the bottom of a shell and set the cactus on it. Then fill the shell with a mixture of half sand and half a combination of very fine pebbles and shredded moss. The pebbles should be no larger than ⅛ inch in diameter. Tap down and water and set in a sunny spot. It will only need to be watered about once a week. Tiny succulents can be used with, or in place of, the cactus too.

To grow some seed in a shell, sprinkle fine pebbles in the bottom, lay down about a half inch of potting soil, and sprinkle it generously with shredded moss. Dampen it down and then sprinkle on seeds. Pat another half inch of soil over seeds and moss. Moisten and keep in the dark until it

PLANTERS (Figure 86)

FIGURE 86 *Clam-shell miniature garden. The interior of the shell is white with ridges edged in brown. There's something nice about seeing sand, shell and cactus joined in one unit.*

begins to sprout, and then set it in the sun where you can watch it grow. Or give it away at this point so someone else can watch it. Some seeds to try are clover, rye, alfalfa, any grass seed, radish, watercress and mustard seed.

Plaques. The shell plaques in Figure 87 were all made with the same basic materials. They are scrap wood ¼″ thick, boxes from a craft store, an assortment of vacation-type shells, white glue, spray adhesive and a resin product called Envirotex. Envirotex is available in craft stores. It's a new product, so if you can't find it drop a note to TAP Plastics, 3011 Alvarado Street, San Leandro, California 94577.

Specific directions for each plaque follow.

PLAQUE *(Figure 87, center)*

This is a box lid measuring 6″ x 3¾″. Lines were penciled in on the bottom of lid, and then it was sprayed with spray adhesive. Soutache braid was cut to fit and pressed onto the surface over the lines. Envirotex was poured over the surface and allowed to set for about twenty minutes, or until it began to set up (congeal). The shells were then laid in place and allowed to dry overnight.

WINDOW BOX *(Figure 87, left)*

The "window" is a box lid measuring 3½″ x 4¼″. A piece of wood for the shelf was sawed from a scrap of ¼″ wood and glued in place with white glue. Envirotex was then poured (in a thin coat) over the bottom of the container. After about

FIGURE 87 *Decorative plaques made of small shells collected on trips to the shore. They are set in liquid resin. Some of the shells have natural hollows that are filled with moss and tiny flowers.*

twenty minutes when the resin began to set up, the shells were pressed into place on the shelves. Shells were selected that had a natural opening for moss and flowers. This arrangement was allowed to dry overnight, and then shreds of moss were placed inside the opening in the shells along with a drop or two of white glue. The stems of flowers and seeds were then positioned in the moss.

SOLO WEED CONTAINER
(Figure 87, right)

The board for this container measured 2½″ x 5″ and was ¼″ thick. After it was cut, the edges were sanded and the whole piece was wiped free of sawdust with a damp cloth. It was then sprayed with a light coat of spray adhesive and the flowers laid in place in center of plaque. (NOTE: The adhesive is not meant to do a total glue job on the flowers but to keep them stationary while the resin is being poured.) The resin was dribbled over the surface of board, including the flowers. After the resin set for twenty minutes, a shell was laid in place over the flowers to appear as though it were a container. It dried for twenty-four hours, and then moss was laid inside the shell and a spray of baby's breath (a dried flower) added.

Flyers and Feathers

At one time there was a Walt Disney character named Dumbo—a likable but rather stupid elephant who knew how to fly. Or at least he could fly when he held a certain feather in his trunk.

Dumbo used to be one of my favorite animals, but I knew (and I guess *he* knew too) that one feather couldn't really keep him aloft. It took a lot of confidence in himself, too, in order to get the job done. But feathers really are amazing inventions. Especially the kind known as flight feathers. I've read that it takes just a few dozen of these fragile-looking things to keep a large bird in the air. It's no wonder they've been described as one of nature's most superbly engineered structures. Over a million separate parts unite in one single feather and come down together, singing in harmony. Underneath the flight feathers, right next to the skin, in fact, is the soft downy plumage that keeps birds cozy and warm. These feathers have done their share of keeping people warm too. No synthetic material can equal the warmth offered by a sleeping bag filled with a duck's underwear. One of my own happiest childhood memories is that of crawling between two feather mattresses in an attic bedroom on my grandparents' farm. There was something incredibly elegant about being the middle portion of a feather sandwich.

Because feathers are so indescribably beautiful, they have been used as the raw material for all kinds of ornamentation. They have been made into towering headdresses, delicate fans, skirts, bonnets and cloaks, and embroidered and women into blankets and tapestries. It's also interesting to note that the Aztecs used feathered mantles in place of money.

SOURCES AND PREPARATION NOTES

The bulk of feathers being sold for art-and-craft purposes today come from fowl that have been raised especially for their feathers. The type seen in art-and-craft stores comes in several shapes and dimensions; some are soft and fluffy while others are clipped and businesslike in appearance. They come in packages containing one to several hundred. Hundreds may seem like a munificent number, but remember that it takes a couple of thousand just to cover up one small barnyard chicken. If you prefer feathers in their natural colors, good sources of supply are the firms that sell Indian craft materials. They offer feathers like pheasant tail, turkey (black and white barred) and rooster tail (iridescent green, blue and black). One of my favorites is the feather of the guinea hen, which is black with symmetrically arranged spots of white.

Anyone with persistence and dedication can collect feathers instead of purchasing them. A surprising number of people are willing to make this effort, myself included. They go where the feathers are—along beaches where sea gulls fly, to farmers with small flocks of chickens, and to large poultry operators. One turkey grower near my home allows people to go out into the fields and gather them. He says this is typical of other growers too. I made inquiries at four major zoos about the possibilities of collecting feathers from their aviaries, but this has to be counted out as a source. They generally don't have the time to gather and clean them, and when they do the feathers are often given to craft groups in veterans hospitals or other such institutions. Cleaning them is a messy business. Maybe it isn't really *that* messy, but I have a personal aversion to it and am always glad when the job is over. Feathers look so degraded and helpless when they're wet that I have trouble relating to them. But in the end I always like the feathers I collect more than the ones I buy. After I get a batch together, I wash them in warm, sudsy water—just as if they were a fine cloth. They are then spread on towels or newspapers to dry. Surprisingly enough, they regain most of their symmetry and fluff. You can help them along by lifting and stirring them and using your fingers to straighten any unruly segments. One lady I know puts feathers into a large sack, ties it shut, and then tosses it into the washing machine on the "delicate" cycle. She makes stunning Christmas wreaths from the pure white feathers.

MOBILE *(Figure 88)*
MATERIALS

This mobile was made with blue craft feathers 3½" to 4" long. The directions are geared to this particular feather and to the irregularities and bulk of the available twig. There's no reason why you have to use the same color or kind of feather. Just adapt the basic directions for the material you choose to

FIGURE 88 *Feather mobile with an overall length of about 20 inches. The slightest air movement makes the feathers move like birds in flight. It is blue, gold and purple.*

work with. You will need approximately twenty feathers, one spool of bright green nylon thread, eight purple glass beads with a large hole, one twig and eight straws. If you don't have natural straw, you can use drinking straws—the slender kind.

1. Cut eight straws into 5″ lengths.

2. Cut feather barbules away from bottom ¾″ of the quill to leave this part of the quill bare. Use a pocket knife or scissors.

3. Push this end up inside a straw. Put in one or two or three, however many fit the straw's dimensions. Wrap this end of straw with thread to bind it together and to add color.

4. On the other end of the straw, place a drop of glue and slip on a bright purple glass bead.

5. Find balancing point of feather wand by balancing it on the rim of a bowl (Figure 89). Wrap a 12″ length of green thread around that point two or three times and knot it. Wrap it tightly, but not so tight that it can't be adjusted later.

6. Suspend twig so it's easy to reach, and tie wand to twig. If wand doesn't balance when you tie it to twig, tap the thread wrapping back and forth until it does. Then put a drop of glue on the wrapping. Continue until all wands are swinging from the twig.

PROCEDURE

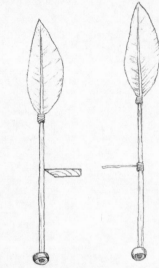

FIGURE 89   *Balancing feather and wrapping it.*

FIGURE 90   *Feather weaving designed with brown yarns, red wooden beads, and brown and white speckled feathers from a guinea hen.*

One coat hanger, one 2-ounce skein of dark brown 4-ply sports yarn, one package of guinea hen feathers, about 4 yards of contrasting light brown yarn, twenty-six red wooden beads with holes large enough to fit over a coat hanger. If you find a few of the beads don't quite fit, just ream them out with a pair of scissors. You will also need a pair of pliers with a wire-cutting attachment.

1. Select and wrap ends of thirty-two feathers in the following manner: Cut a 2″ length of light brown yarn and lay over quill end of feather so it forms a loop (Figure 91, left). Cut another length of the same yarn 10″ long and wrap feather and loop together. Knot (Figure 91, right).

2. With pliers, cut a coat hanger on both sides of the junction of its hook. Bend into a circle and refine it with the help of pliers. You will have a circle approximately 12″ in diameter. Blunt the cut ends a little so the yarn won't snag.

3. Thread beads and feathers onto hanger. Put on three beads, one group of eight feathers; three more beads, another group of eight feathers, etc., until you have four bunches of eight feathers. End with three beads. Push together at top of circle at the side away from the opening in hanger.

4. Wrap hanger with yarn, using a buttonhole kind of wrap (Figure 92). Wrap until circle is tightly packed with yarn, then bend ends of hanger into a hook, one on each side. Join one hook over

WEAVING (Figure 90)

MATERIALS AND TOOLS

PROCEDURE

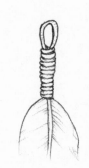

FIGURE 91 *Making a loop and wrapping the loop and quill together.*

FIGURE 92 *Wrapping hanger with yarn.*

the other and wrap and cover junction with yarn.

5. Cut thirty-six lengths of main color yarn 60″ long; fold in half and attach to bottom of circle with a simple macrame knot (see Figure 42). Decorate hanging yarn by sliding remaining red beads up the yarn and tying a knot beneath them.

NECKLACE *(Figure 93)* The feathers are gold and red, so I chose a bright orange yarn to bring the colors together. Use the following directions for a design, but substitute any colors for the yarn, beads and feathers.

MATERIALS Six yards 4-ply woolen yarn, twenty-five feathers 4″ to 6″ long, an assortment of beads. (NOTE: If you want to follow this pattern exactly, you will need ninety-six wooden beads and thirty-six ceramic beads with a large hole.) There are some odd tin beads in this necklace too, but I don't remember what kind of cast-off they came from. They're not available commercially, but they're not a necessary part of the necklace either. I put them in because I liked the idea of hearing their sound when the necklace moved.

PROCEDURE 1. Cut three lengths of yarn 27″ long and nine lengths 14″ long.

2. Make a "needle" out of one end of your yarn lengths by dipping it into white glue and shaping it into a point. After it hardens, begin to thread beads.

3. Place beads on each 27″ length of yarn in the

FIGURE 93   *Necklace made of yarn, beads and feathers in orange, brown, red and gold. This necklace can also be worn tied around the upper leg just above the knee.*

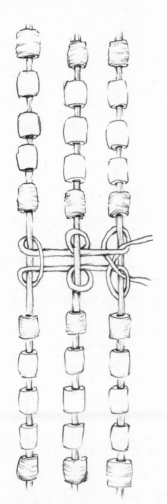

following way: Thread four wooden beads, one ceramic; four wooden, one ceramic; four wooden, two ceramic; four wooden, two ceramic; four wooden, two ceramic; four wooden, one ceramic; four wooden, one ceramic; four wooden. Center the beads. There will be about 6″ remaining on each end of the yarn.

4. Prepare feather dangles by folding seven of the 14″ strands in half. Lay out the three lengths of beaded yarn, one above the other. Place a folded 14″ strand over top length and tie a simple macrame knot between the ceramic beads and set of wooden beads (Figure 94). Knot the second strand, and then the third, beginning in this way to tie the three strands together. Tie an extra knot at bottom. Continue to join, placing one dangle after each grouping of beads.

5. Thread two ceramic beads on end of each dangle and slide several feathers up inside the beads. Wrap yarn once around the feathers below the beads. Tie a knot and drop on one spot of glue.

* * *

The presents in this book, whether they were made of stones, sand or stalks of grain, all have one thing in common—their firm connections to the earth. In that way, they share a universal beauty

FIGURE 94 *Joining three necklace strands.*

totally separate from whatever skills a craftsman's hands might have brought to them.

With an elegant show of humility which most of us could adopt, the earth continually makes and distributes gifts without expectations of thank-you cards or favors in return. As a result, many of its finest efforts go unnoticed—not because they are common or insignificant but because we grow so accustomed to their presence that we no longer even see them, let alone recognize their beauty.

I don't think it would hurt at all if we tried to find ways to thank the earth for being so patient and generous. Not necessarily by elaborate ceremonies but by a series of thoughtful, continuing gestures. It might make up in part for past neglect. Just for starters, here's an idea you might want to consider:

Take some seeds—any seeds that come your way. Throw them as high as you can in places where the earth has been wounded by cement, highway salt or earth-moving machinery. Let the wind determine where the seeds should fall. Keep on spreading seeds in this fashion and dream about the time when cracks in sidewalks and spaces in used-car lots will be filled with apple trees, pomegranates and sunflowers. Cover the earth with thank-you seeds.

Sources of Supplies and Information

CLAY

AMACO

4717 West 16th Street
Indianapolis, Indiana 46222
(A variety of clays plus clay supplies and equipment.)

DYEING

Lamb's End
16861 Hamilton
Highland Park, Michigan 48203
(Dyes, mordants, variety of fibers, undyed yarn, books. Free price list.)

Natural Dye Supplies
P.O. Box 7
Pelham, New York 10803
(Chemicals for mordanting. Free price list.)

Indiana Botanic Gardens
626 177th Street
Hammond, Indiana 46325

(Herbs and dried plants for making dyes. Price list and a catalog-almanac filled with herbal information, 25 cents.)

EGGS

Rock Mountain Farm
Box 167
Mosier, Oregon 97040

Kathryn Johnson
Bushkill Drive, R.D. 2
Easton, Pennsylvania 18042

FEATHERS

Gettinger Feather Co.
38 West 38th Street
New York, New York 10018
(Feathers by the pound, or by the hundreds. Price list.)

Grey Owl Indian Craft Supplies
150–02 Beaver Road
Jamaica, New York 11433
(Wide variety of sizes, both dyed and natural. Catalog 25 cents.)

GOURDS

Carl Odom
Pinola, Mississippi 39149
(Gourds and gourd seeds—request price list.)

American Gourd Society
Box 274
Mt. Gilead, Ohio 43338
(A society that, among other things, publishes a magazine called *The Gourd.* $2.50 gives you a membership and a subscription.)

Nichols Herb and Rare Seeds
1190 North Pacific Highway
Albany, Oregon 97321
(Seeds for ornamental corn, gourds, herbs, flowers for dried foliage. Large, fascinating catalog.)

INDIAN CRAFT SUPPLIES AND INFORMATION

Grey Owl (See listing under Feathers.)
(Horn, antler, bone, tusk, claw, beads, skins.)

Robert's Indian Craft Supplies
211 West Broadway Street
Anadarko, Oklahoma 73005
(Beads, shells, horse hair, bells, gourds. Price list free.)

Indian Arts & Crafts Board
U.S. Department of the Interior
Washington, D.C. 20240
(They publish two Source Directories—No. 1 and No. 2—which list "Indian and Eskimo Individuals Marketing Native American Arts and Crafts." Free. They also publish a bibliography on native American arts and crafts.)

PAPER

Aiko's Art Materials Import
714 North Wabash
Chicago, Illinois 60611
(Booklet 1″ thick, 3½″ x 6¾″ of samples of handmade paper carried. $3.00.)

SEEDS

Walnut Acres
Penns Creek, Pennsylvania 17862
(Seeds to sprout and eat, and Beale's Famous Seed Sprouter. Free catalog, which also lists grains, honey, cereals, nuts, etc.)

SHELLS

Grey Owl (See listing under Feathers.)

SKIN (Leather)

Grey Owl (See listing under Feathers.)
(Rawhide, rawhide lacing and thong, tom-tom heads, fur, tooling leather, etc.)

Tandy Leather Co.
5945–47 W. North Avenue
Chicago, Illinois 60639
(Wide selection of leather and leather supplies. Free catalog.)

SOAPSTONE

Arts and Crafts, Inc.
9520 Baltimore Avenue
College Park, Maryland 20740
(Send for price list.)

WEEDS, SEEDS AND PODS FOR DRY FOLIAGE

The Golden Unicorn
22 Rustic Drive, Howell Township
Lakewood, New Jersey 08701
(Sample price list is free. Full catalog is 50 cents.)

The Fir Tree
P.O. Box 130
Mi-Wuk, California 95346
(Seeds, cones, pods, beans, grasses, acorns, etc. Send for price list.)

Floral Art
Main Street
Dennis, Massachusetts 02638
(Miscellaneous dried foliage, skeletonized leaves, pods. Catalog free.)

WILDFLOWERS TO GROW

Clyde Robin
P.O. Box 2091

Castro Valley, California 94546
(Huge catalog, $1.00, lists a "Special Roadside Mixture" of wild-
flowers; has tree seeds, shrubs, vegetables, etc.)

The Three Laurels
Route 3, Box 15
Marshall, North Carolina 28753
(Free price list of wildflowers, plants, etc.)

Gardens of the Blue Ridge
Ashford, McDowell County
North Carolina 28603
(Wildflowers, trees, etc. Catalog free.)

Nichols Herb and Rare Seeds
(See listing under Gourds. Their catalog lists "Everlasting Flowers"
and even has a leaflet to tell you how to sell them once they're
grown.)

Books and Other Printed Sources of Information and Enjoyment

CLAY

Barford, George. *Clay in the Classroom*. Worcester, Mass.: Davis Publications, Inc., 1963.

Denver Art Museum. *Pueblo Indian Pottery Making*. Leaflet No. 6, 1930, reprinted July 1967. (Includes information on open-firing methods. Available from Grey Owl. See Sources of Supplies and Information.)

Johnston, Randolph Wardell. *The Book of Country Crafts*. Cranbury, N.J.: A. S. Barnes, 1964.

Wahlman, Maude. "An African Potter at Work." Field Museum of Natural History Bulletin, Volume 43, No. 8. Chicago, September 1972. (A good description of one method of open firing.)

DYEING

Adrosko, Rita J. *Natural Dyes in the United States*. Washington, D.C.: Smithsonian Institution, 1968. Also in paperback as *Natural Dyes and Home Dyeing*, New York: Dover Publications, 1971.

Lesch, Alma. *Vegetable Dyeing*. New York: Watson-Guptil Publications, Inc., 1971.

See also Randolph Wardell Johnston's *The Book of Country Crafts,* under Clay.

GOURDS

Bailey, L. H. *The Garden of Gourds.* American Gourd Society, 1958. This book is available from the Gourd Society, Box 274, Mt. Gilead, Ohio 43338.

LEATHER

See Gardi's *African Crafts and Craftsmen,* below.

Denver Art Museum. *Parfleches and Other Rawhide Articles.* Leaflet 77–78, December 1936. Reprinted July 1967. (Available from Grey Owl. See Sources of Supplies and Information.)

See Wulff's *Traditional Crafts of Persia,* below.

W. Ben Hunt. *Golden Book of Crafts and Hobbies.* New York: Golden Press, 1957.

(On page 6–7 there is an account of how to make your own rawhide from a fresh hide.)

PAPER

Dard, Hunter. *Paper Making in the Classroom.* Peoria, Ill.: Manual Arts Press, 1931.

Mason, John. *Paper Making as an Artistic Craft.* Leicester, England: Twelve by Eight Press, 1963.

PLANTS, WILD AND CULTIVATED

Anderson, Edgar. *Plants, Man and Life.* Berkeley, Calif.: University of California Press, 1952.

Leopold, Aldo. *A Sand County Almanac*. New York: Ballantine Books, Inc., 1949.

ROCKS AND GEMS

Macfall, Russell P. *Gem Hunter's Guide*. New York: Thomas Y. Crowell, 1969.

Pearl, Richard M. *American Gem Trails*. New York: McGraw-Hill Book Co., 1964.

Sinkankas, John. *Gemstones of North America*. New York: Van Nostrand Reinhold, 1959.

SHELLS

Jordan, Emil Leopold. *Hammond's Guide to Nature Hobbies*. Maplewood, N.J.: C. S. Hammond & Co., Inc., 1953.

Morris, Percy A. *A Field Guide to the Shells*. Boston: Houghton-Mifflin Co., 1951.

Taxay, Don. *Money of the American Indians*. New York: Nummus Press, 1970.

SPECIAL BOOKS ABOUT NATIVE AND PRIMITIVE ARTISTS AND CRAFTSMEN

Allen, Edward. *Stone Shelters*. Cambridge, Mass.: M.I.T. Press, 1969.

The Beaver, Magazine of the North. "Eskimo Art"—a whole issue is devoted to Eskimo artists, their history, materials, examples of ancient and contemporary art, etc. Winnipeg, Canada: Hudson's Bay Company, Autumn 1967.

Dickey, Roland F. *New Mexico Village Arts*. Albuquerque, N.M.: University of New Mexico Press, 1949, 1970.

Gardi, Rene. *African Crafts and Craftsmen*. New York: Van Nostrand Reinhold Co., 1970.

Ishimoto, Tatsuo. *The Art of the Japanese Garden*. New York: Crown Publishers, Inc., 1958.

Quimby, George I. *Indian Life in the Upper Great Lakes*. Chicago: University of Chicago Press, 1960.

Tanner, Clara Lee. *Southwest Indian Arts and Crafts*. Tucson, Ariz.: University of Arizona Press, 1968.

Trowell, Margaret. *African Design*. New York: Praeger Publishers, 1960.

Wheat, Margaret M. *Survival Arts of the Primitive Paiutes*. Reno, Nev.: University of Nevada Press, 1967.

Whiteford, Andrew Hunter. *North American Indian Arts*. New York: Western Publishing Co., Inc., 1970.

Wulff, Hans E. *The Traditional Crafts of Persia*. Cambridge, Mass.: M.I.T. Press, 1966.

Index

Beverly Plummer   A folk singer and a student for many years of all the folk arts, Beverly Plummer is, with her husband, associated with a wilderness camp in Wisconsin. She is also a writer whose articles have appeared in *Venture, Parents' Magazine, Woman's Day* and a number of Sunday supplements. Her previous book, *Give Every Day a Chance*, was published in 1970. She and her husband have recently bought a 29-acre forest in Wisconsin, in which they will design and build their own home.